Key Stage 3 Science

Spectrum

Chemistry

Key Stage 3 Science

Spectrum

Chemistry

Andy Cooke

Jean Martin

CAMBRIDGE
UNIVERSITY PRESS

Series editors	Andy Cooke
	Jean Martin
Consultant	Sam Ellis
	Doug Wilford
Authors	David Acaster
	Derek Baron
	Trevor Bavage
	Andy Cooke
	David Fagg
	Kevin Frobisher
	Jean Martin
	Mick Mulligan
	Doug Wilford

CAMBRIDGE UNIVERSITY PRESS
Cambridge, New York, Melbourne, Madrid, Cape Town, Singapore, São Paulo, Delhi

Cambridge University Press
The Edinburgh Building, Cambridge CB2 8RU, UK

www.cambridge.org
Information on this title: www.cambridge.org/9780521549226

© Cambridge University Press 2004

First published 2004
5th printing 2009

Printed in Dubai by Oriental Press

A catalogue record for this publication is available from the British Library

ISBN 978-0-521-54922-6 paperback

Material in this book was previously published in *Spectrum Year 7 Class Book* (pp. 53–104), *Spectrum Year 8 Class Book* (pp. 51–96) and *Spectrum Year 9 Class Book* (pp. 50–106).

Cover design by Blue Pig Design Co
Page make-up and illustration by Hardlines Ltd, Charlbury, Oxford

Contents

About *Spectrum Chemistry*

This *Spectrum* Class Book covers what you will learn about science and scientists in Key Stage 3 chemistry. It is split into twelve **Units**. Each Unit starts with a page like this:

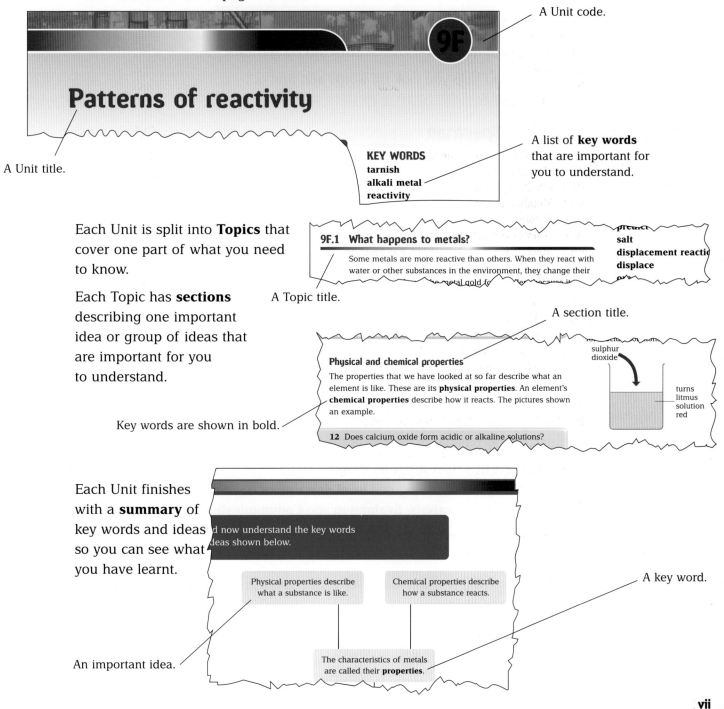

A Unit code.

Patterns of reactivity

A Unit title.

KEY WORDS
tarnish
alkali metal
reactivity

A list of **key words** that are important for you to understand.

Each Unit is split into **Topics** that cover one part of what you need to know.

9F.1   What happens to metals?

Some metals are more reactive than others. When they react with water or other substances in the environment, they change their

predict
salt
displacement reactio
displace

A Topic title.

Each Topic has **sections** describing one important idea or group of ideas that are important for you to understand.

A section title.

Physical and chemical properties
The properties that we have looked at so far describe what an element is like. These are its **physical properties**. An element's **chemical properties** describe how it reacts. The pictures shown an example.

12 Does calcium oxide form acidic or alkaline solutions?

sulphur dioxide

turns litmus solution red

Key words are shown in bold.

Each Unit finishes with a **summary** of key words and ideas so you can see what you have learnt.

d now understand the key words deas shown below.

Physical properties describe what a substance is like.

Chemical properties describe how a substance reacts.

A key word.

An important idea.

The characteristics of metals are called their **properties**.

Icons

 Telling you where to look in the Class Book to help with activities.

 Asking questions about what you have just learnt.

 Asking questions that help you think about what you have just learnt.

 Asking questions that might need some research to answer.

At the end of the book

At the end of the book you will find:

- pages 156 to 163 to help you with **scientific investigations**;

- a **glossary/index** to help you look up words and find out their meanings.

Other components of *Spectrum*

Your teacher has other components of *Spectrum Chemistry* that they can use to help you learn. They have:

- a **Teacher file CD-ROM** full of information for them and lots of activities of different kinds for you. The activities are split into three levels: **support**, **main** and **extension**. Some of the activities are **suitable for homework**.

Also available by year:

- an **assessment CD-ROM** with an **analysis tool**. The CD-ROM has **multiple choice tests** to find out what you know before you start a Unit and for you to do during or after a Unit. It also has some end of year **SAT-style tests**.

And free on the web available at www.cambridge.org/spectrum:

- general guidance documents on aspects of the Science Framework;

- **investigation checklists**, **investigation sheets** – writing frames to help with structuring investigations, and **level descriptors** covering **Planning**, **Observation**, **Analysis**, **Evaluation** and **Communication**;

- **mapping grids** for the **Five Key Ideas**, **Numeracy**, **Literacy**, **ICT**, **Citizenship** and **Sc1**;

- **flash cards** for use as a revision aid or for card chases using the Years 7, 8 and 9 key words;

- **Five Key Ideas cards** for use as a revision aid and to build giant concept maps.

Acids and alkalis

In this unit we shall be finding out about acids and alkalis and how to recognise them. We shall also look at some uses of acids and alkalis and at neutralisation reactions.

KEY WORDS
acid
sour
hydrochloric acid
hazard
corrosive
dilute
harmful
irritant
risk
alkali
sodium hydroxide
extract
indicator
full-range universal
   indicator
pH scale
neutral
react
neutralisation
salt
indigestion

7E.1 What acids and alkalis are like

Acids are all around us

It is amazing how many things around us contain **acids**. Some acids are in the food we eat. We use acids to make things work properly and to make all sorts of useful items. Some acids are harmless, but others are very dangerous.

Fruit or drinks made from fruit often contain acids. They have a tangy, sharp taste. We say acids taste **sour**.

1 Look at the picture. Write down a list of substances that contain acids.

2 Write down:

   a <u>one</u> word that best describes the acid taste of lemon juice;

   b the name of the acid that gives lemon juice this taste.

3 **a** What is the name of the other acid in limes and lemons?

   b What disorder does this acid help to prevent?

Limes and lemons taste sour because they contain citric acid. Lemons and limes prevent scurvy because they contain vitamin C. Vitamin C is also an acid, but it is a very weak acid.

LIME JUICE

Some acids are dangerous

Not all acids are the same. Fruit juice is not dangerous but there are some acids that can be risky to use. Substances like **hydrochloric acid** have their own **hazard** warning sign. Hazard warning signs let people know that they need to be careful. People who use hazardous chemicals must protect themselves and others.

The particular hazard of hydrochloric acid is that it is **corrosive**. This means that it will immediately attack your skin and start eating it away. The hazard warning sign shows this.

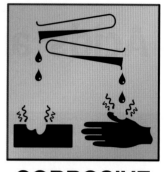

CORROSIVE

Hydrochloric acid – you need to be very careful.

 4 Look at the hazard warning sign for hydrochloric acid. What does the word 'corrosive' mean?

If you get hydrochloric acid on yourself, you should wash the area with lots of water. When you mix acid with water, we say that you **dilute** it. This makes the acid less dangerous.

You also need to be careful with dilute hydrochloric acid. Dilute acids are **harmful** or **irritant**, so we use a black cross to warn people about their risks.

This is the sign for an irritant.

 5 If you spill hydrochloric acid on your skin:

    a what can happen?

    b what do you need to do?

    Explain your answers.

 6 Why must you always wear eye protection when you use hydrochloric acid?

This is the sign for a harmful substance.

About alkalis

The group of chemicals shown in the picture are not acids but they do react with acids. These substances are **alkalis**. When acids and alkalis react, their properties are cancelled out.

We make soap using alkali and oils. Your skin contains oils. When you get alkali on your skin, your skin oils react with the alkali and your skin feels soapy as it dissolves away. We call the wound a chemical burn.

All these substances contain alkalis.

7 Make a list of household substances which contain alkalis.

Some alkalis are safe to use. Others, such as **sodium hydroxide,** are just as dangerous as the strongest acids.

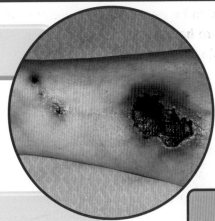

Alkalis can be dangerous. These burns were caused by caustic soda. Caustic soda is also known as sodium hydroxide.

8 What is the hazard symbol on the bottle of bleach?

9 What do you need to do if bleach accidentally gets into your eyes?

10 Why do you need to show the label to the doctor if you accidentally swallow some bleach?

 THICK BLEACH CONTAINS SODIUM HYDROXIDE.
Irritating to eyes and skin.
Warning Do not use with other products.
May release dangerous gases (chlorine).
Store upright in a cool safe place away from babies, children and animals.
Avoid contact with skin and eyes.
In case of contact with eyes, rinse immediately with plenty of water and seek medical advice.
After contact with skin wash immediately with plenty of clean water.
IF SWALLOWED SEEK MEDICAL ADVICE IMMEDIATELY AND SHOW THIS CONTAINER LABEL.

Uses of acids and alkalis

We find acids and alkalis in many natural substances.
The chemical industry makes millions of tonnes of acids
and alkalis every year.

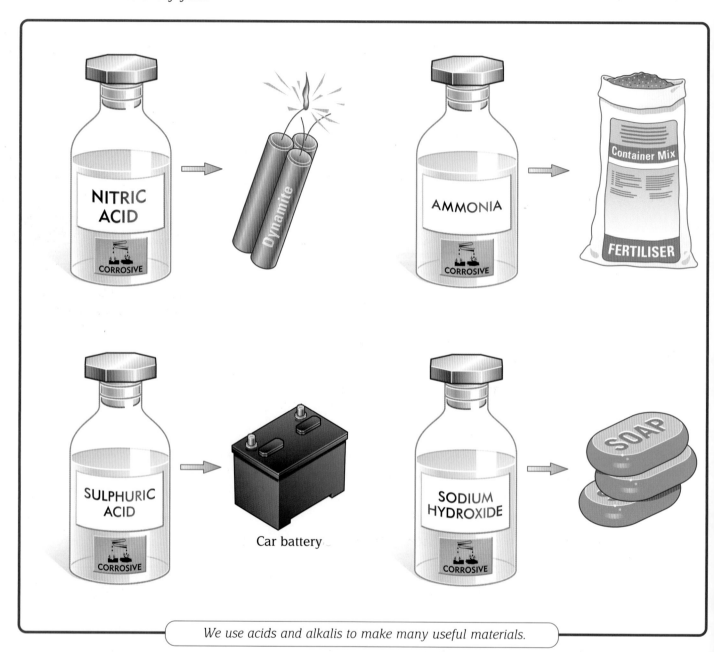

We use acids and alkalis to make many useful materials.

 11 Name the acid or alkali used to make:

   a car batteries;

   b explosives;

   c soap;

   d fertilisers.

7E.2 Telling acids and alkalis apart

Sodium hydroxide, hydrochloric acid, lemonade and water are all colourless liquids. They <u>look</u> the same, but they are really very different substances.

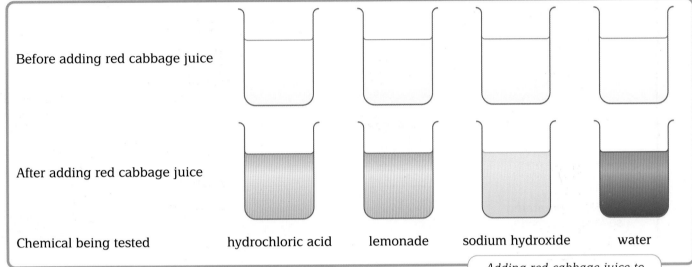

Before adding red cabbage juice

After adding red cabbage juice

Chemical being tested   hydrochloric acid   lemonade   sodium hydroxide   water

Adding red cabbage juice to four colourless liquids.

1 Look at the pictures. What colour does red cabbage juice turn when added to:

    a hydrochloric acid;   **b** lemonade;

    c sodium hydroxide;   **d** water?

2 Is lemonade an acid or an alkali? Explain your answer.

We can use the colour change of red cabbage juice to show if a substance is an acid or alkali. We can use juices from some other plants too. We call plant juices **extracts**.

● Red cabbage juice and beetroot juice are vegetable extracts.

● Blackcurrant juice is a fruit extract.

● Litmus is extracted from a lichen.

All these extracts change colour to show or <u>indicate</u> whether a substance is an acid, an alkali or neutral. So we call them **indicators**.

3 Name <u>two</u> indicators that can be made from vegetables.

4 What is an extract?

5 Find out what lichen is.

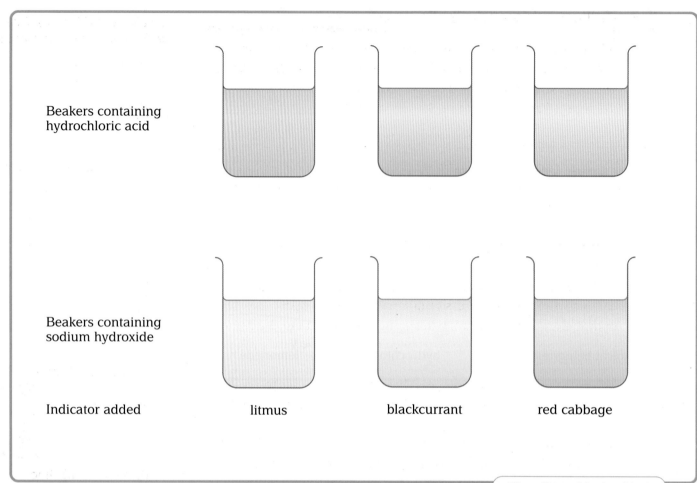

Beakers containing hydrochloric acid

Beakers containing sodium hydroxide

Indicator added   litmus   blackcurrant   red cabbage

The effect of hydrochloric acid and sodium hydroxide on some indicators.

6 Is sodium hydroxide an acid or an alkali?

7 What colour do the following indicators turn when added to hydrochloric acid?

 a blackcurrant;

 b litmus;

 c red cabbage.

8 What colour do the following indicators turn when added to sodium hydroxide?

 a blackcurrant;

 b litmus;

 c red cabbage.

9 What do some plant extracts do that makes them useful indicators?

7E.3 Universal indicator and the pH scale

All the indicators that we have looked at so far only tell us if a substance is an acid or an alkali. Lemonade and hydrochloric acid have the same effect on all these indicators, but they have a very different effect if you spill them on your skin.

1   Luke tells his teacher that he can tell the difference between lemonade and hydrochloric acid very easily. 'All you have to do is taste them.' If you were Luke's teacher what would you tell him?

Full-range universal indicator is a special type of indicator that is made by combining lots of different indicators together. We can use it to show if something is acid, alkaline or neutral. But we can also use it to show if something is strongly acidic like hydrochloric acid or weakly acidic like lemonade. In the same way, we can use it to tell whether an alkali is weak or strong.

2   Water is a neutral substance. What colour do you get when you add a few drops of universal indicator to a test-tube of water?

Scientists actually measure the strengths of acids and alkalis on a scale from 0 to 14 known as the **pH scale**. They match the indicator colours to the numbers on the pH scale.

On the pH scale numbers between 0 and 6 are for acids and numbers from 8 to 14 are for alkalis. The number 7 is neither acid nor alkali – we say that it is **neutral**.

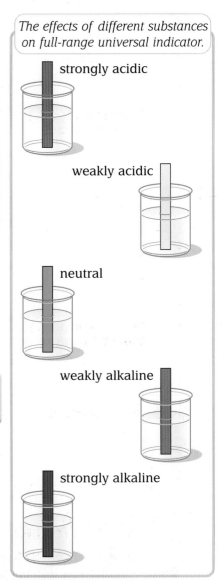

The effects of different substances on full-range universal indicator.

strongly acidic

weakly acidic

neutral

weakly alkaline

strongly alkaline

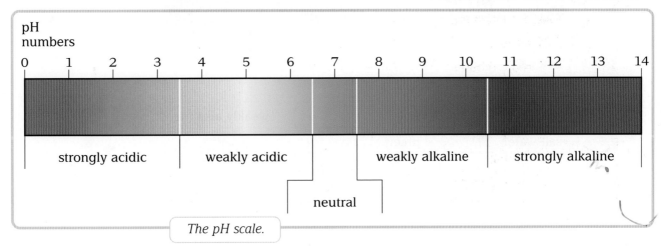

The pH scale.

pH numbers

0 1 2 3 4 5 6 7 8 9 10 11 12 13 14

strongly acidic   weakly acidic   weakly alkaline   strongly alkaline

neutral

3 What do you think the pH of each of the following substances will be?

　a Strongly acidic hydrochloric acid;

　b Weakly acidic lemonade;

　c Strongly alkaline sodium hydroxide.

4 What colour will full-range universal indicator go if you add it to the following substances?

　a potassium hydroxide, pH = 12;

　b soda water, pH = 5;

　c sulphuric acid, pH = 2.

5 A beaker of concentrated hydrochloric acid has a pH of 1.

　a What colour will full-range universal indicator turn if it is added to the beaker?

　b Is concentrated hydrochloric acid strongly or weakly acidic?

6 A group of pupils tested a range of chemicals but they lost some of their results and so they could not complete the table. To help them, answer the questions.

Substance	Colour with full-range universal indicator	pH	Type of substance
nitric acid	red	1	strongly acidic
vinegar		5	
ammonia	purple		
sodium bicarbonate	blue		weakly alkaline
salt water	green	7	

　a What colour was the full-range universal indicator in vinegar?

　b What is a possible value for the pH value of ammonia?

　c What type of substance is salt water?

　d What is the possible value for the pH of sodium bicarbonate?

7E.4 Neutralisation and the rainbow experiment

When an acid and an alkali are mixed together a chemical reaction happens. The acid **reacts** with the alkali to cancel it out. This reaction is called **neutralisation**.

About neutralisation

During a neutralisation reaction the pH of a solution changes. This is because the acid and the alkali cancel each other out. This produces a neutral substance called a **salt**. Water is also produced. Neutralisation is an important chemical reaction.

acid + alkali → salt + water

If exactly the right amount of acid is added to an alkali the solution produced is neutral. However, if too much acid is added the solution will become acidic.

1 What happens when too little acid is added to an alkali?

The rainbow experiment is an example of a neutralisation reaction actually taking place. In this experiment, you put a washing soda crystal into a test-tube full of water. Washing soda is an alkali. Its scientific name is sodium carbonate.

You add hydrochloric acid to almost fill the test-tube, then a few drops of full-range universal indicator.

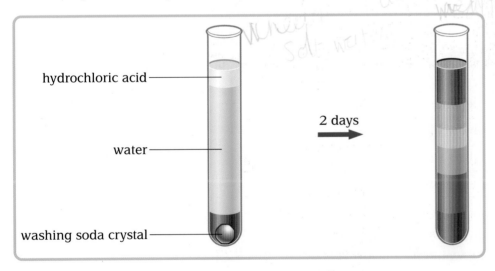

hydrochloric acid

water

washing soda crystal

2 days

2 **a** What colour is the solution close to the washing soda crystal?

   b Are washing soda crystals acid or alkaline?

3 **a** After 2 or 3 days what is the pH of the solution at the top of the test-tube?

b Part of the solution has turned yellow. What will the pH of the solution be here?

c Both the yellow section and the top of the test-tube are acidic. What is the difference between them?

4 In the blue part of the solution, is there more acid present or more alkali?

In the rainbow experiment the hydrochloric acid has slowly moved down the test-tube. The washing soda crystal has dissolved and the alkaline solution has moved up the test-tube. Neutralisation takes place where the two solutions meet.

5 After 2 or 3 days there is a small part of the solution which is green. Is this part of the solution acidic, alkaline or neutral?

6 Andrew tried to do the rainbow experiment, but after 2 or 3 days his test-tube was completely purple. What can he do to get a rainbow?

The rainbow experiment.

What happens with other acids and alkalis?

There are many examples of neutralisation reactions with acids and alkalis. In each of these a salt is produced, as well as water. The salt produced depends on which acids and alkalis are used.

We can describe what has happened by using a <u>word equation</u>.

> hydrochloric acid + sodium hydroxide → sodium chloride + water

The name of the salt depends on the acid and the alkali:

- hydrochloric acid gives <u>chloride</u>
- sodium hydroxide gives <u>sodium</u>

to give the salt <u>sodium chloride</u>.

7 If we used potassium hydroxide instead of sodium hydroxide what salt would we make?

7E.5 Where neutralisation is important

Neutralisation is a very important reaction in our daily lives.

Curing indigestion

Indigestion is often caused by too much acid in the stomach. You can take medicine to neutralise this acid. Some contain a weak alkali called magnesium hydroxide. Other indigestion cures contain magnesium carbonate or sodium bicarbonate. These neutralise acids but also make carbon dioxide, which is a gas.

1 What causes indigestion?

2 Sodium hydroxide solution has a pH of 14.
Why can't you use sodium hydroxide to cure indigestion?

Sarah and her class decided to investigate some indigestion remedies to see if they were any good. Look at their table of results.

Tablet	Cost per tablet	Amount of acid neutralised	Amount of gas produced	Time taken to neutralise the acid
Brand A	3p	25 cm^3	none	3 minutes
Brand B	4p	20 cm^3	none	10 minutes
Brand C	5p	30 cm^3	15 cm^3	2 minutes
Brand D	1p	10 cm^3	28 cm^3	1 minute
Brand E	8p	40 cm^3	15 cm^3	2 minutes

3 **a** Which tablet neutralises the most acid?

   b Which is the cheapest tablet?

   c Which tablet works more slowly than all the others?

4 **a** What is the name of the gas produced?

   b What is the name of <u>one</u> substance which makes this gas?

5   What happens if you take an indigestion tablet that makes a lot of gas?

6   Which indigestion tablet do you think you should use? Explain your answer.

7   Sarah found it hard to measure the amount of acid that Brand E neutralised because the tablets were red.
    Why is it hard to do the experiment with red tablets?

Other uses of neutralisation reactions

Toothpaste

Your mouth is full of bacteria. These feed on any food left in your mouth. These bacteria then produce acid in your mouth. The acid can attack your teeth, making them decay. When you brush your teeth the alkali in toothpaste neutralises the acid. This helps to protect your teeth.

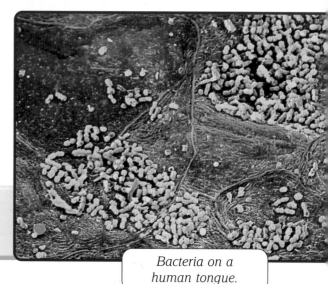

8   Your saliva is slightly alkaline. What effect will saliva have on the amount of acid in your mouth?

Bacteria on a human tongue.

9   Dentists recommend chewing sugar-free gum after meals. Why do you think this helps reduce tooth decay?
    (Hint: Chewing causes lots of saliva to be produced.)

Making cakes rise

Baking powder is an ingredient in some cake recipes. It contains both an acid and an alkali. The alkali is called bicarbonate of soda. When the acid neutralises the bicarbonate of soda the gas carbon dioxide is produced. It is this gas that produces the bubbles in sponge cakes.

The pH of this toothpaste is 8 because it contains bicarbonate of soda.

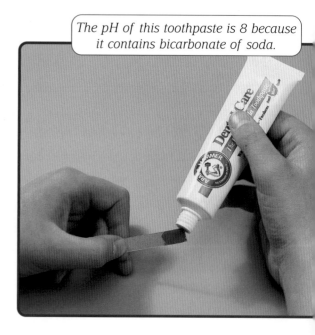

Acid rain

Some factories and power stations pollute the air with gases that cause acid rain. Rainwater dissolves these acid gases so that its pH is lower than 7. Acid rain can harm the environment.

Soil treatment

The pH of soil is different in different places. In some areas the soil is too acidic for plants to grow well and therefore lime is added. Lime raises the pH because it is an alkali. Lime is also called calcium oxide. It will neutralise some of the acid in the soil. This means that the pH of the soil is raised, making it less acidic. Plants can now grow well.

Often, calcium carbonate is added to lakes because it neutralises the acid that comes from the rain water.

 10 Write down <u>three</u> examples of uses of neutralisation.

 11 Potatoes grow well on Jim's farm, which has soil with a pH of 5.5. He decides to add lime to his soil so he can grow broccoli instead.

    a Do potatoes grow better in acid or alkaline soil?

    b Does broccoli grow better in acid or alkaline soil?

 12 a What are the advantages and disadvantages of adding lime to the soil?

    b Why do you think Jim decided to grow broccoli?

You should now understand the key words and key ideas shown below.

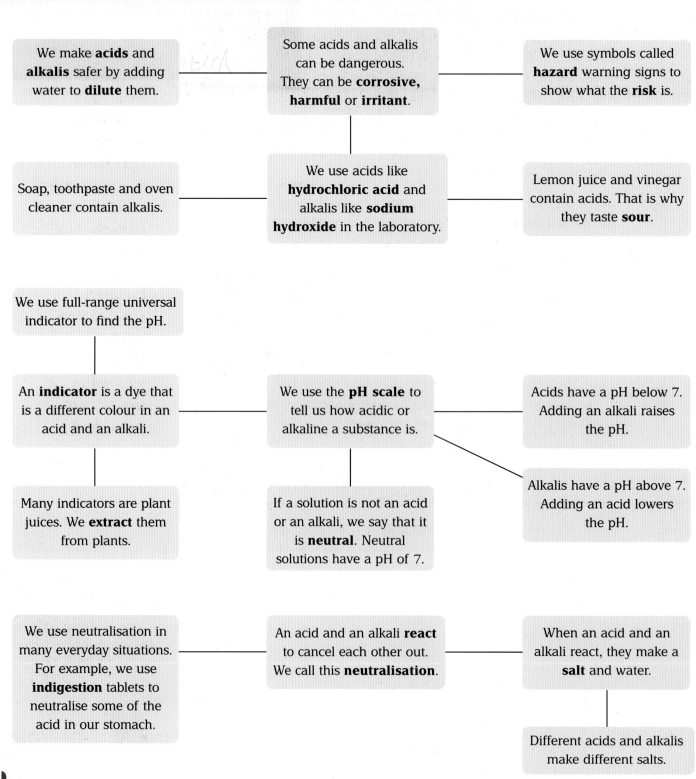

We make **acids** and **alkalis** safer by adding water to **dilute** them.

Some acids and alkalis can be dangerous. They can be **corrosive, harmful** or **irritant**.

We use symbols called **hazard** warning signs to show what the **risk** is.

Soap, toothpaste and oven cleaner contain alkalis.

We use acids like **hydrochloric acid** and alkalis like **sodium hydroxide** in the laboratory.

Lemon juice and vinegar contain acids. That is why they taste **sour**.

We use full-range universal indicator to find the pH.

An **indicator** is a dye that is a different colour in an acid and an alkali.

We use the **pH scale** to tell us how acidic or alkaline a substance is.

Acids have a pH below 7. Adding an alkali raises the pH.

Alkalis have a pH above 7. Adding an acid lowers the pH.

Many indicators are plant juices. We **extract** them from plants.

If a solution is not an acid or an alkali, we say that it is **neutral**. Neutral solutions have a pH of 7.

We use neutralisation in many everyday situations. For example, we use **indigestion** tablets to neutralise some of the acid in our stomach.

An acid and an alkali **react** to cancel each other out. We call this **neutralisation**.

When an acid and an alkali react, they make a **salt** and water.

Different acids and alkalis make different salts.

Simple chemical reactions

In this unit we shall be studying some chemical reactions. We shall look at what happens when acids react with metals and when acids react with carbonates. We shall also find out more about burning.

KEY WORDS
chemical reaction
hydrogen
reactants
products
corrosion
word equation
carbonate
carbon dioxide
limewater
oxygen
burning
combustion
oxide
fuel
explosion
fire triangle
fossil fuel

7F.1 Chemical reactions

In a **chemical reaction**, new substances are made. Chemical reactions are happening all around you. They happen in your kitchen, in your garden and inside your body. Chemical reactions break down the food that you eat into simple substances. More chemical reactions then build the simple substances up into different things like flesh and bone.

If you heat an egg, the substances in it change into new substances. Chemical reactions have happened.

The runny inside goes hard. The taste of the egg changes too.

If you heat ice, it changes to water and then to steam. Ice, water and steam are all the same chemical. You have changed it from a solid to a gas but you haven't made a new substance. So this is <u>not</u> a chemical reaction.

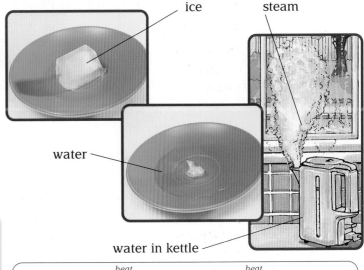

ice   steam

water

water in kettle

1. Write down an everyday example of a chemical reaction.
2. What happens in a chemical reaction?
3. Why isn't changing ice into water a chemical reaction?

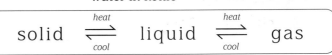

$$\text{solid} \underset{cool}{\overset{heat}{\rightleftharpoons}} \text{liquid} \underset{cool}{\overset{heat}{\rightleftharpoons}} \text{gas}$$

7F.2 Reactions between acids and metals

In this topic we are going to look at what happens when you add an acid to a metal. Look at the picture.

1 Write down <u>two</u> changes that you can see.

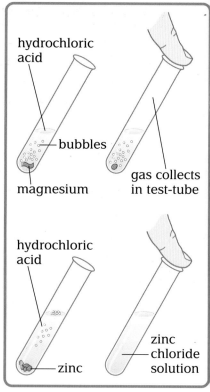

In Olwen's first experiment, she added an acid to magnesium. Then she tested the gas given off with a lighted splint.

The 'pop' showed that the gas was **hydrogen**.

In this experiment, magnesium and hydrochloric acid <u>react</u> together. So we call them **reactants**.

Magnesium chloride and hydrogen are <u>produced</u> in the reaction. So we call them **products**.

There is less metal at the end of the reaction because it has been changed into a new substance. A word to describe the disappearance of the metal is **corrosion**.

You can describe a chemical reaction by writing a **word equation**. You write all the reactants on the left and all the products on the right. The arrow shows the direction of the reaction.

> reactants → products

So the word equation for Olwen's first experiment is:

> magnesium + hydrochloric acid → magnesium chloride + hydrogen

For her second experiment, Olwen used magnesium and sulphuric acid. She tested the gas produced and found out that it was hydrogen too.

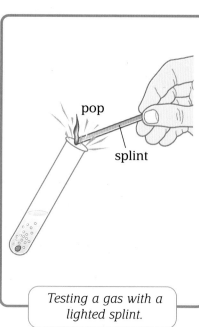

Testing a gas with a lighted splint.

2 a What did Olwen do to test for hydrogen?
b What happened?

3 For Olwen's second experiment:
a write down the reactants **b** write down the products
c use the reactants and products to write a word equation.

4 Olwen noticed that there was less magnesium at the end of the experiment. Write down <u>one</u> word that describes the disappearance of the magnesium.

7F.3 Reactions between acids and carbonates

Washing soda, baking powder and many rocks contain **carbonates**. Geologists test rocks to see if the rocks contain carbonates. If a rock fizzes when a geologist adds acid, the rock contains carbonates.

 1 Write down <u>one</u> example of a carbonate.

Carbonates fizz when an acid is added to them because they give off a gas called **carbon dioxide**.

If you test carbon dioxide with a lighted splint, it does not 'pop'. The flame goes out.

 2 Do carbonates fizz because of a chemical reaction? Explain your answer.

Limestone is made of calcium carbonate.

If you bubble carbon dioxide through **limewater**, the limewater goes cloudy.

 3 Write down the gas produced when acids and carbonates react.

4 Write down <u>two</u> tests for carbon dioxide.

5 Which of the two tests do you think is the better test for carbon dioxide?

— limewater

Carbon dioxide is the only gas that makes limewater go cloudy.

Using carbonates at home

To make light fluffy cakes we often use a mixture called 'baking powder'. The ingredients in baking powder are tartaric acid and sodium bicarbonate. They don't react when they are dry.

When tartaric acid and sodium bicarbonate react, they make carbon dioxide. The trapped bubbles get bigger as the cake cooks.

So the cake rises until it goes solid.

 6 What gas does baking powder produce?

7 How does baking powder help in making cakes?

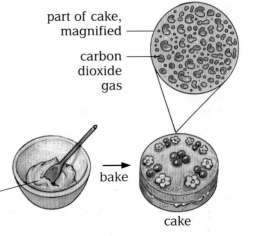

part of cake, magnified

carbon dioxide gas

baking powder in the cake mix

bake

cake

7F.4 Reactions when substances burn

Oxygen reacts with most substances. When this reaction is fast and gives out heat and light, we call it **burning** or **combustion**. When substances burn in air they react only with the oxygen in the air.

 1 What gas is always used in burning?

Look at the pictures. They both show gases being burnt, but with differing results.

b Burning acetylene in oxygen.

a Burning natural gas in air.

 2 Write down <u>two</u> differences between the flames.

3 Why are the two flames different?

 4 Which flame do you think is the hotter? Explain your answer.

5 Why is the welder wearing eye protection in the pictures?

The general word equation for burning is:

substance + oxygen → substance **oxide**

Many substances will burn in oxygen. You have to be careful because the reactions can produce a lot of heat and light. Also, it is dangerous to breathe in the fumes. Non-metal oxides are acidic so they can irritate your lungs.

Iron (a metal).

Iron oxide.

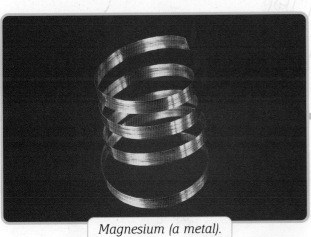

Magnesium (a metal).

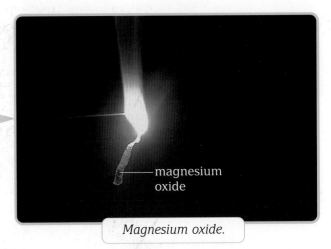

magnesium oxide

Magnesium oxide.

Carbon (a non-metal).

Carbon dioxide.

 6 What do we call the substances that are made when elements burn in oxygen?

7 Write word equations for the three reactions shown above.

7F.5 Reactions when fuels burn

We burn some substances to give us the energy we need for heating and cooking. We call them **fuels**.

Hydrogen gas burns in air to form water. When hydrogen burns, lots of energy is released. If hydrogen is mixed with a lot of air, it burns very quickly and produces an **explosion**.

1 Why don't we use hydrogen as a fuel in our homes?

2 Look at the word equation.

> hydrogen + oxygen → water

Write down:

a the reactants;

b the product.

Hydrogen is the lightest gas. It was once used to fill huge airships that carried passengers.

3 Find out why hydrogen airships were not used for long and why they were all dismantled.

The fire triangle

Three things are needed to make a fire. We can think of these three things as the three sides of a triangle – the **fire triangle**.

- We need oxygen from the <u>air</u>.
- We need a <u>fuel</u>.
- We need <u>heat</u> to set fire to the fuel.

Then the fuel burns to produce light and more heat.

If we take away one of these three 'sides', the fire goes out.

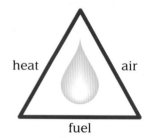

4 Write down <u>three</u> things that are needed for a fire to burn.

5 Look at the three pictures of ways of fighting fires. They all work by removing one of the three 'sides' needed for a fire. Explain how each one works.

Fire-fighters use powerful water jets to cool and soak substances that might continue to burn.

Fire extinguishers often contain carbon dioxide, a heavy gas, or a foam. They smother a fire by keeping the air out.

Bulldozers can be used to remove trees in a strip.

The substances produced when fuels burn

We use a lot of energy every day for lighting, heating, cooking and entertainment, and to transport us to work or school.

Most of this energy is produced by burning **fossil fuels**. We burn fossil fuels in power stations and at home.

Natural gas, butane, oil, petrol and paraffin are fossil fuels. They contain only hydrogen and carbon. So when they burn, they produce oxides of hydrogen and carbon.

The word equation for burning a fossil fuel is:

Paraffin lamp.

fossil fuel + oxygen → carbon dioxide + water

6 Look at the pictures. For each picture, write down the fuel used.

7 Write down the name of a gas that is

   a used in burning **b** made when a fuel burns.

8 Natural gas is also called methane. Write a word equation for what happens when methane burns.

7F.6 Looking at a candle burning

Wax is a very difficult substance to burn. It has to be turned into a gas before it will burn. Like ice, wax takes a lot of heat to melt it and then to turn it into a gas.

$$\text{solid} \xrightarrow{\text{heat}} \text{liquid} \xrightarrow{\text{heat}} \text{gas (vapour)}$$

$$\text{wax} \xrightarrow{\text{heat}} \text{molten wax} \xrightarrow{\text{heat}} \text{wax vapour}$$

- When you light a candle, the heat from the flame melts the wax.
- The wick soaks up the molten wax, in the same way that blotting paper soaks up water.
- The flame heats the small amount of liquid wax on the wick.
- This turns the liquid wax into wax vapour.
- The wax vapour mixes with air and burns.
- This produces carbon particles that glow yellow in the heat.
- As more air mixes in, the carbon also burns.

1   What does the candle use for fuel?

2   How does the fuel get to the flame?

Putting a candle out

3   Explain why blowing hard on a candle puts it out.
Which side of the fire triangle is being removed?

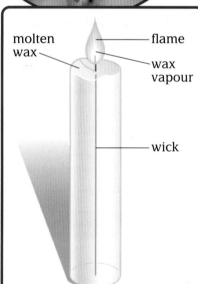

molten wax — flame — wax vapour — wick

Another way of putting a candle out

This is what happened when Ahmed put a jar over a burning candle:

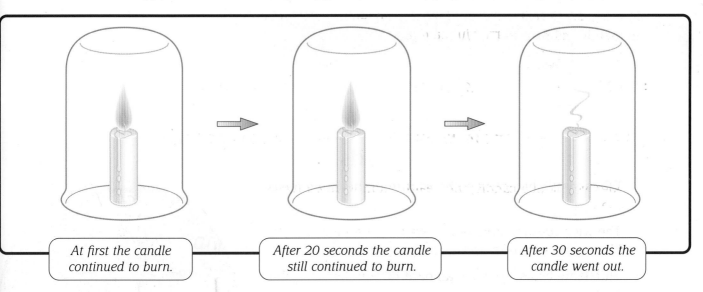

At first the candle continued to burn.

After 20 seconds the candle still continued to burn.

After 30 seconds the candle went out.

4 Describe what happens to the flame after the jar has been put over the burning candle.

5 What new substances are trapped under the jar?

6 Why do you think the candle went out? (Hint: Think about what gets used up when a candle burns.)

7 Ahmed did the experiment again, but he used a bigger jar. What difference do you think this made?

8 Look at the pie chart. Is all the air used up in burning? Explain your answer.

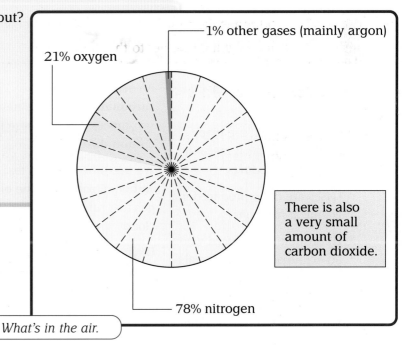

1% other gases (mainly argon)

21% oxygen

There is also a very small amount of carbon dioxide.

78% nitrogen

What's in the air.

You should now know these key words and key ideas.

Key words

chemical reaction	carbonate	oxide
hydrogen	carbon dioxide	fuel
reactants	limewater	explosion
products	oxygen	fire triangle
corrosion	burning	fossil fuel
word equation	combustion	

Key ideas

In a **chemical reaction** new substances are produced.

Substances that are used up in a chemical reaction are called **reactants**.

Substances that are made during a chemical reaction are called **products**.

Gases are often produced in chemical reactions.

Hydrogen is produced when an acid reacts with a metal. The metal is used up. We call this **corrosion**.

We test for hydrogen using a lighted splint. You hear a 'pop' if there is hydrogen.

We can describe a chemical reaction with a **word equation**.

An acid reacts with a **carbonate** to produce new substances. One of these is **carbon dioxide**.

We use **limewater** to test for carbon dioxide. It is the only gas that turns limewater cloudy.

Oxygen reacting with a substance is called **burning** or **combustion**.

The **oxide** of a substance is made when a substance burns.

Fuels release energy when they burn.

An **explosion** is very fast burning.

A fire needs oxygen from air, fuel and heat to burn. We show this as a **fire triangle**.

Fossil fuels contain only carbon and hydrogen. They release carbon dioxide and water when they burn.

Particle model: solids, liquids and gases

In this unit we shall look at the way our ideas about substances have changed. We shall also learn how to use these ideas to explain things that we see in laboratory experiments and in everyday life.

KEY WORDS
matter
material
substance
evidence
theory
model
particle
solid
liquid
gas
states of matter
flow
Brownian motion
random
particle model of
   matter
kinetic theory
vibrate
compress
diffusion
pressure
expansion
heat conduction

7G.1 Looking at and thinking about substances

All the stuff we see and feel in the world we call **matter** or **material**. Types of matter are called **substances**. Substances include water, gold, leaves, brick, hair and acids. There are millions of different types of substances.

1   Write down the names of <u>ten</u> substances that are part of the matter in the room with you now.

You can study substances in lots of different ways. You can do experiments with substances to see what they do. You might be surprised how some substances behave.

2   Look at the pictures. Choose <u>one</u> of the experiments shown in the pictures. Write down your idea to explain what you see.

When you do experiments, you write down observations and measurements. All of the observations and measurements are called **evidence**. You can use evidence to help you to explain things. Scientists work in this way too.

You can smell the gas given off by the air freshener

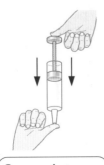

Some substances can be squashed

0 °C

100 °C

Some substances get bigger when you heat them

190.0 g

003.6 g

024.3 g

Some substances are heavier than others

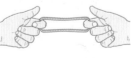

Some substances get longer

3 Write down <u>two</u> things that scientists do to collect evidence.

4 **a** Imagine using a very powerful microscope to look inside the substance that you chose in question 2. What do you think it is like inside? Discuss your ideas with another pupil.

b If you have changed your mind about your answer to question 2, write down your new idea. Don't cross out the old idea.

7G.2 Thinking about theories

Some scientists collect evidence about matter. They use their imaginations to think of ideas to explain the evidence. We call these ideas **theories**. Sometimes scientists make pictures in their minds as part of their theory.

Scientists discuss and argue about ideas all the time.

1 What is a theory?

Scientists discuss their theories and argue about them. They don't always agree. The scientists often need to look for more evidence. Then they try to see if their theory also explains the new evidence. If it doesn't, they change their theory, or even make a new theory altogether. When they think that a theory explains all the evidence, the group of ideas and pictures in their imagination is called a **model**.

2 What do scientists call theories that explain all the evidence?

3 Why do you think scientists argue about their ideas?

Making a theory is very similar to what happens as a detective tries to solve a crime. The detective collects clues. She makes up theories, and discusses and argues with other detectives. She looks for more clues. When she finds more clues, she may change her theory. She keeps doing this until the evidence can be explained and the criminal is caught.

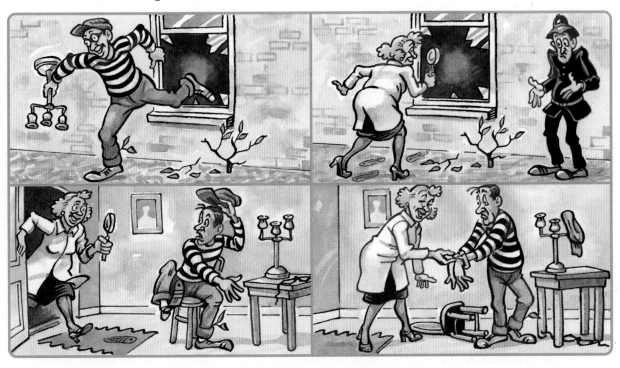

4 How is the work of a detective like that of a scientist? Make a list of the things that are the same.

A theory about matter

We call very small pieces of matter **particles**. The idea that matter is made of very small particles is very old. Over 2000 years ago in ancient Greece, a scientist called Democritus said that everything was made of small particles.

To explain what he meant, Democritus asked people to imagine that he had a bar of gold and a magic knife. The magic knife could cut any substance. When he cut the bar of gold in half, the two halves were smaller than the whole bar. As he kept cutting, the pieces got smaller and smaller. After many cuts, he would get a very small particle that the knife would not cut.

Democritus believed that everything could be cut this way and that all matter is made of particles. He argued with other thinkers. Some agreed with him but others did not.

Democritus.

5 Write a letter to a relative about Democritus and his particle idea. Say whether or not you agree with Democritus's theory, and why.

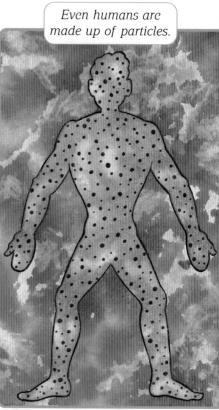

Breaking down substances always makes particles.

7G.3 A closer look at solids, liquids and gases

You probably know how important grouping and sorting is in everyday life! To make it easier to study and understand the world, scientists also sort things into groups.
For example, scientists divide living things into two groups: plants and animals. Then they divide these very large groups into other smaller groups.

Another way that scientists use to sort substances is to group them into **solids**, **liquids** and **gases**. Scientists call these three groups the three **states of matter**.

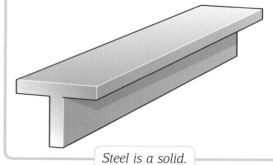

Steel is a solid.

1 Write down the <u>three</u> states of matter.

Solids have a definite shape and volume. They are very difficult to squash. Some solids seem to be heavy for their size. Steel is hard.

2 A man jumps up and down on a large stone.
Does the stone change shape?

Water is a liquid.

Liquids take up the shape of the container they are in and keep the same volume. They are difficult to squash. Liquids can **flow**, which means they can be poured and can move through gaps. Generally, liquids aren't very heavy for their size.

3 Water can be poured easily, but ice cannot.
What states of matter do water and ice belong to?

4 Milk is poured from a bottle into a jug. Does the shape of the milk change?

Gases fill any container. Gases flow like liquids. They are very easy to squash. Most gases are light for their size.

5 Water and gas come through pipes into houses. Why can both water and gas be delivered in this way?

Nitrogen dioxide is a brown gas.

6 Write down <u>three</u> properties of:
a solids **b** liquids **c** gases.

7G.4 Some evidence for the particle theory

You read about Democritus's theory about particles on page 27. Lots of people discussed his theory and argued about it. The problem was that evidence was hard to find. Eventually the idea of particles was forgotten for hundreds of years.

But now, the idea of particles is widely accepted by scientists. Many scientists collected evidence over many years. Now scientists can even take photographs of particles using X-rays and electron beams. The particles are very, very small; they are much too small for us to see in any other way.

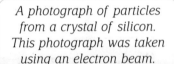

A photograph of particles from a crystal of silicon. This photograph was taken using an electron beam.

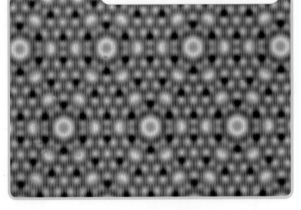

1 What new techniques gave scientists direct evidence for particles?

2 What can you say about the size of particles in the air?

Robert Brown and small moving things

In 1827, a Scottish biologist called Robert Brown used a microscope to look at pollen grains in water. The pollen grains jiggled around and followed a zigzag path. He thought that pollen grains were living, moving creatures. What was very strange was that 100-year-old pollen grains did the same jiggling. Scientists called this type of movement **Brownian motion**. They kept discussing whether the pollen was alive or dead.

Robert Brown (1773–1858).

Some scientists looked at other substances, such as smoke, dust, soot grains and scrapings of pencil leads. These scientists also saw Brownian motion. The small bits these scientist looked at could not be alive. So, scientists had to make up a new theory to explain Brownian motion.

3 Eventually, scientists agreed that pollen grains weren't alive even though they were moving. Write down <u>one</u> piece of evidence that they used to support this idea.

In 1877, a French scientist called Desaulx argued that very small, invisible air particles moving in a random way caused Brownian motion. **Random** means you can't tell which way something will move next. Look at the picture to see what Desaulx meant.

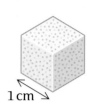

A 1 cm³ cube of air contains about 30 million million million particles (30 × 10¹⁸).

The path of a pollen grain that is jiggling about.

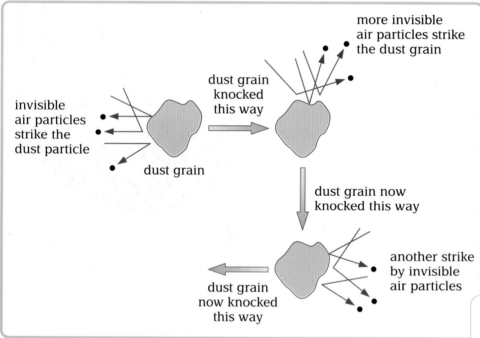

A dust grain is hit by invisible air particles, making it jiggle about in a random way.

4 What did Desaulx think caused Brownian motion?

In 1900, another scientist, F. M. Exner, found that smaller granules moved faster. He also showed that they moved faster when they were warmer. In 1905, Albert Einstein calculated the sizes and speeds of the particles at different temperatures. He used mathematics to draw exact charts of Brownian motion. This work was part of the reason he won the 1921 Nobel Prize for Physics.

5 What happens to the movement of particles as the temperature rises?

6 Did Exner's discoveries provide evidence for either of the two theories about Brownian motion? Explain your answer.

7 It is a bright sunny day. In a boy's bedroom, the sun shines through a gap in the curtains. The boy sees dust particles in the strong beam of light. The bits of dust seem to jiggle around even though there is no wind. Try to explain what is happening to the bits of dust.

We can see how Brown, Desaulx, Exner and Einstein developed Democritus's theory about particles. They gathered evidence and suggested theories. They changed their theories when they found new evidence.

The theory changed until it had five main ideas. These five ideas are called the **particle model of matter**.

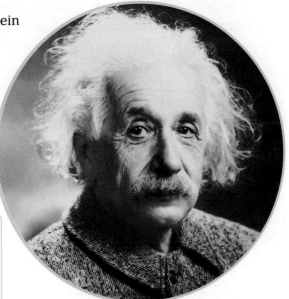

1 All matter is made up of particles.

2 The particles can be of different sizes.

3 The particles move around by themselves in a random way.

4 The particles attract each other.

5 The hotter the substance, the faster the particles move.

Albert Einstein (1879–1955). He proved that the particle model of matter explained Brownian motion.

Some scientists call this model the **kinetic theory**. Kinetic is the Greek word for <u>movement</u> (scientists often use Greek words).

8 Pretend you are writing an email, back through time, to Robert Brown. Explain why you think pollen grains are not living creatures even though they jiggle around when you look at them under a microscope. You need to mention the particle model of matter in your email.

7G.5 Using the particle model

In this topic we will see how the particle model can explain many of the observations we have made about matter.

Particles in crystals

Many solids are made up of crystals. Crystals have straight edges.

Look at the straight edges of these crystals.

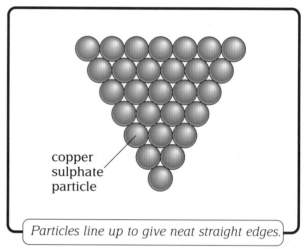

copper sulphate particle

Particles line up to give neat straight edges.

1 Write down the names of <u>two</u> crystals.

2 Do all the crystals have sharp, straight edges?

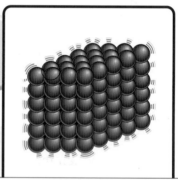
In solids, the particles vibrate while staying in their places.

3 Use the particle model to explain why both small and large crystals of the same substance have the same shape.

Particles in solids, liquids and gases

Solids, liquids and gases are all made up of particles.

In solids, forces of attraction hold the particles together. The particles **vibrate** but they don't change place with the particles next to them. Vibrate means to move from side to side. There is very little space between the particles.

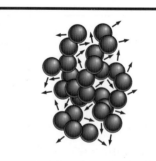
In liquids, the particles still vibrate. They are attracted to each other less than in a solid. This means they can swap places with each other.

4 Write down <u>two</u> differences between the particles in a solid and a liquid.

5 Liquids take the shape of their containers and they can be poured. Use the particle model to explain these properties.

In a gas the particles are far apart and are moving very fast. There is very little attraction between the particles and they move about freely.

6 In which one of solids, liquids and gases:

   a are the particles closest together?

   b is the attraction between particles the greatest?

   c can particles move about the most freely?

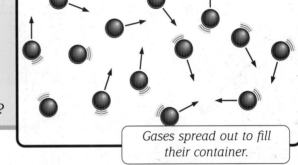

Gases spread out to fill their container.

Compressing solids, liquids and gases

The scientific word for 'squashing' is **compressing**. Solids and liquids are difficult to compress. Gases are easy to compress. We can use the particle model to explain these differences.

7 Explain why gases are easy to compress, but liquids and solids are not.

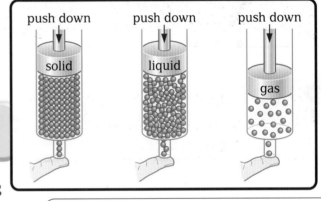

Only gases have enough space between their particles for the particles to be squeezed together.

Melting, boiling, freezing and condensing

We use heat to melt a solid. Heat makes the particles move faster. When the particles get enough energy, they start to overcome the attractive forces between them. The particles can then start to swap places – the solid melts to form a liquid.

If we continue to heat the particles, they get even more energy and move faster still. Spaces open up between the particles until a gas is formed. The liquid has boiled.

Condensing is the reverse of boiling. Freezing is the reverse of melting.

8 When you heat up a solid, what happens to the particles?

9 When you cool a gas, what happens to the speed of the particles?

Diffusion

Look at the pictures. They show how some substances seem to spread out without any help from air currents, water currents or stirring. We call this spreading out **diffusion**.

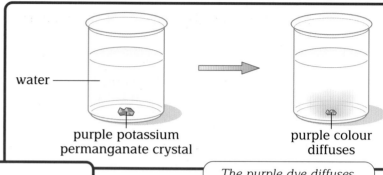

water —

purple potassium permanganate crystal

purple colour diffuses

The purple dye diffuses through the water.

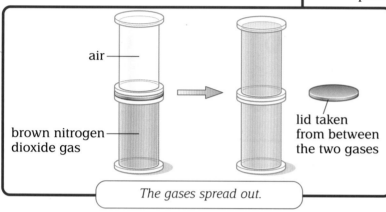

air —

brown nitrogen dioxide gas

lid taken from between the two gases

The gases spread out.

10 What is diffusion?

11 Look at the pictures. Write down <u>one</u> example of diffusion of:

   a a gas   **b** a dissolved solid.

12 Look at the pictures of the particles in the brown gas and the air. Describe what happens when you remove the lid between the two gases.

We can use the particle model to explain diffusion.

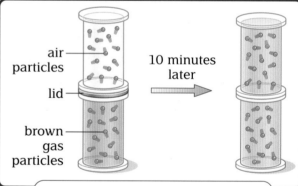

air particles

lid —

brown gas particles

10 minutes later

The gas particles are moving, so they mix. We say that they diffuse.

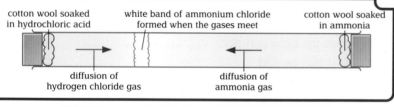

cotton wool soaked in hydrochloric acid

white band of ammonium chloride formed when the gases meet

cotton wool soaked in ammonia

diffusion of hydrogen chloride gas

diffusion of ammonia gas

The two transparent gases diffuse. They form a white cloud when they meet. Both of the gases have particles that are moving.

13 Use the particle model to explain what is happening in the glass tube.

14 A girl is doing some cooking in the kitchen. The cooking smells soon reach her brother's room. He calls down to ask what she is cooking. Explain <u>one</u> way that the smell could have got up to her brother's room.

15 A balloon full of air goes down slowly, even though the knot at the bottom of the balloon is airtight. After a week all the air has escaped from the balloon. Use the particle model to explain why this happens. Write down what you think. Draw a diagram to help explain how the air particles got out of the balloon.

The can crushing experiment

Peter heated a can containing a little water. The water boiled and the steam drove out most of the air from inside the can. Peter screwed the lid back on the can and left it to cool. As the can cooled it collapsed.

The particle model can help us to explain what happens in Peter's experiment. The steam forces out the air particles that were inside the can. As the steam cools, it turns back to water. The can now has mainly liquid water inside it.

This means that there are more air particles hitting the outside of the can than are hitting the inside. The outside air particles batter the can inwards and crush it. The **pressure** or pushing force of the particles on the outside of the can is greater than the pressure on the inside.

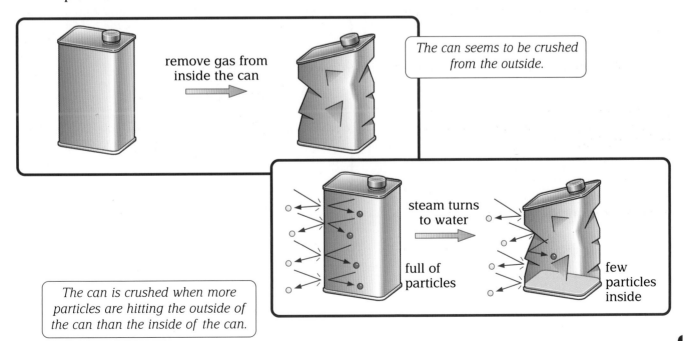

remove gas from inside the can

The can seems to be crushed from the outside.

steam turns to water

full of particles

few particles inside

The can is crushed when more particles are hitting the outside of the can than the inside of the can.

7G.6 More uses of the particle model

Liquids and gases flow but solids don't

In solids, the forces of attraction between the particles are too big to allow the rows of particles to break up and flow. In liquids, the forces are smaller and so they can flow when they are poured. In gases, the attractive forces between particles are slight. Gas particles can flow out of a beaker without the beaker even being tipped up.

1   What is the difference in the forces between the particles in solids, in liquids and in gases?

2   Explain why solids cannot flow.

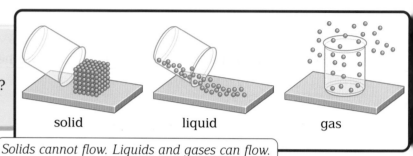

solid   liquid   gas

Solids cannot flow. Liquids and gases can flow.

Expansion and particles

Expansion means getting bigger. Most substances expand when you heat them. Solids expand slightly, liquids expand more, and gases expand a lot.

3   Which type of substance expands the most: a solid, a liquid or a gas?

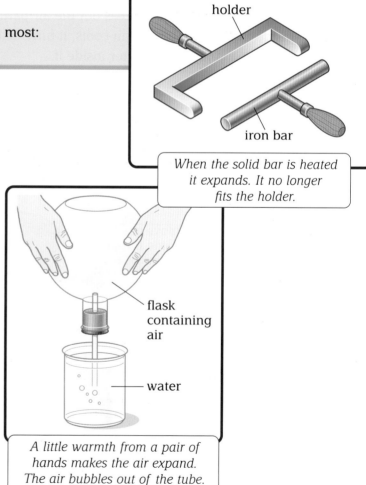

holder

iron bar

When the solid bar is heated it expands. It no longer fits the holder.

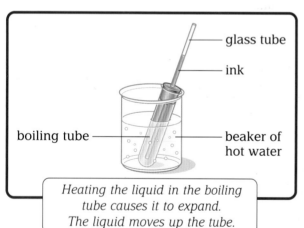

glass tube

ink

boiling tube

beaker of hot water

Heating the liquid in the boiling tube causes it to expand. The liquid moves up the tube.

When a substance expands, the particles do <u>not</u> get bigger. Instead, the particles speed up and move further apart, so they take up more space. The attractive forces between the particles are smaller in gases and liquids, so gases and liquids expand more than solids.

flask containing air

water

A little warmth from a pair of hands makes the air expand. The air bubbles out of the tube.

4 What happens to the particles when a substance expands?

 5 Using the particle model, try to explain why a gas expands more than a solid. Use diagrams to help you.

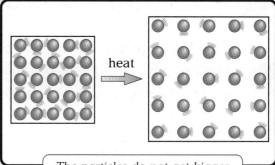

The particles do not get bigger, they move further apart.

Heat conduction in solids

Look at the picture. The spoon gets hot because heat from the coffee travels through the metal of the spoon. We say that heat is conducted through the spoon.

Particles at high temperatures move and vibrate faster than those at lower temperatures. The fast vibrating particles collide and hit their slower neighbours, making these vibrate faster too. The faster vibrations pass up the metal in the spoon and eventually the top of the spoon gets hot. **Heat conduction** has taken place.

The top of the spoon gets hot.

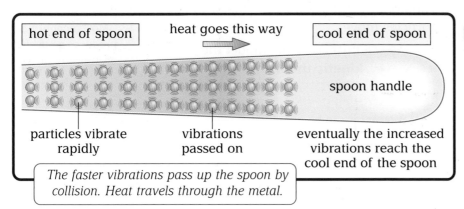

The faster vibrations pass up the spoon by collision. Heat travels through the metal.

 6 What do we call the way heat travels through a solid?

 7 Write down <u>three</u> other examples of heat conduction in solids. Describe how the particle model explains what happens in your examples.

You should now understand the key words and key ideas shown below.

When scientists have collected **evidence** they try and make pictures in their minds. They use their imaginations and make up lists of ideas that might explain the evidence. We call this making theories. When a **theory** can explain the evidence, the group of ideas and pictures is called a **model**.

We often describe **matter** or **materials** as **substances**.

The **particle model of matter**
1 All matter is made up of **particles**.
2 The particles can be of different sizes.
3 The particles move around by themselves in a **random** way.
4 The particles attract each other.
5 The hotter the substance the faster the particles move.
Some scientists call this model the **kinetic theory**.

Random movement of particles causes spreading out of particles. We call this **diffusion**.

Random movement of particles is called **Brownian motion**.

Movement of particles produces a pushing force or **pressure** on a surface.

Expansion means getting bigger. Solids expand slightly; liquids expand more and gases expand a great deal. During expansion the particles move further apart. The particles don't get bigger.

Substances can be sorted into three groups: **solids**, **liquids** and **gases**. These three groups are called the three **states of matter**.

Solids don't **flow** because the forces between the particles are strong. Gases and liquids flow because the forces between particles are much weaker.

Solids and liquids are difficult to **compress**, but gases compress easily. This is because gases have large gaps between the particles.

In **solids**, strong forces hold the particles together so they **vibrate**, but do not change places. There is little space between particles.

In **liquids**, the particles are still attracted to each other but they move faster. They swap places with each other. There is a little more space between the particles.

In a **gas**, there is little attraction between the particles so they move freely. The particles are far apart and moving very fast.

Heat travels in solids by **conduction**. The vibration of the particles is passed through a solid as the particles knock into each other.

Solutions

In this unit we shall be learning about solutions. We shall explore which solids and liquids make solutions and we will see how we can separate solids and liquids from solutions.

KEY WORDS
mixture
dissolve
solution
solute
solvent
soluble
insoluble
pure
filtration
evaporation
sodium chloride
particles
condensation
condenser
distillation
chromatography
attracted
chromatogram
saturated solution
solubility

7H.1 Mixing solids and liquids

If you have you ever spilt water on your exercise book during a science experiment you may have noticed something strange happen. The ink from your pen may 'run' but the pencil doesn't. This is because the water dissolves the ink but does not dissolve the pencil. You can see this in the picture.

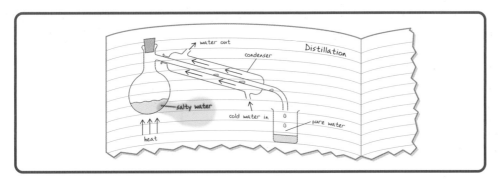

Making solutions

If you mix salt into a beaker of water the salt seems to 'vanish'. Sand just sinks to the bottom.

Both the beakers now contain **mixtures** of a solid and a liquid. However, there is one important difference. The salt **dissolves** in the water but the sand doesn't.

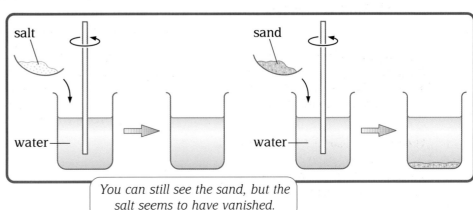

You can still see the sand, but the salt seems to have vanished.

When the salt dissolves in the water it makes a **solution**. In the salt solution the salt and water are given special names:

- the salt is called the **solute** – it is the solid that dissolves to make the solution;

- the water is called the **solvent** – it is the liquid that dissolves the salt.

The salt dissolves in water. We say that salt is **soluble** in water. When a solid dissolves it is called soluble. Sand does not dissolve in water. We say that sand is **insoluble** in water. When a solid will not dissolve it is called insoluble.

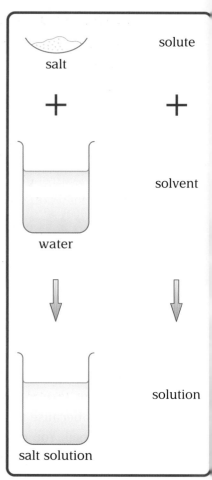

solute

salt

+

solvent

water

solution

salt solution

1 Write down the name of the solute and the solvent used to make a salt solution.

2 Some chalk is mixed with water. How can you tell if the chalk is soluble or insoluble?

3 If sand were soluble in water, what would happen to the world's beaches?

Everyday mixtures

A bottle of mineral water is labelled 'pure' to tell us that nothing has been added to it. However, this 'pure' mineral water contains many different minerals dissolved in water and is really a mixture. To a scientist something is **pure** only when it contains just a single substance and not a mixture of substances.

Mixtures are found everywhere. Here are some mixtures you may come across:

- mineral water is a mixture of water and dissolved minerals;

- a cup of coffee is a mixture of hot water, milk and dissolved coffee (and possibly sugar);

- milk is mainly a mixture of water, sugar, protein and fat;

- sea water is mainly a mixture of water and dissolved salt.

mineral water

cup of coffee

bottle of milk

sea water

4 Look at the picture of the everyday mixtures.
Name <u>two</u> mixtures found in the kitchen.

5 Which of the following are mixtures?
a sugar; **b** a cup of tea; **c** pure water.

Separating mixtures of solids and liquids

We have seen how you can make two completely different mixtures of solids in liquids:

● a mixture of sand and water; ● a salt solution.

We use different ways to get the solids back from both of these mixtures. We say that we use different <u>separation techniques</u>. The separation technique we use depends on whether the solid has dissolved or not.

First let's look at the sand and water mixture. The sand is insoluble and has not dissolved in the water. The sand is separated from the water using **filtration**.

Now let's look at the salt solution. The salt is soluble and has dissolved in the water. Filtering won't work because the salt solution will just go straight through the filter paper. Instead, the salt is separated from the water by **evaporation**.

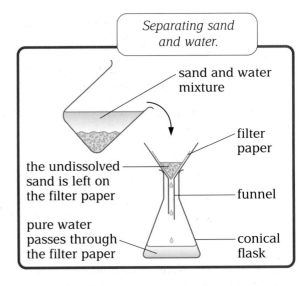

Separating sand and water.

sand and water mixture

filter paper

the undissolved sand is left on the filter paper

funnel

pure water passes through the filter paper

conical flask

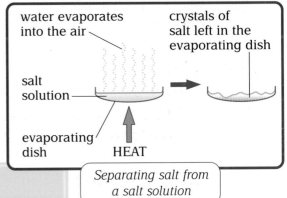

water evaporates into the air

crystals of salt left in the evaporating dish

salt solution

evaporating dish

HEAT

Separating salt from a salt solution

6 Name the separation technique used to separate:

a sand from a mixture of sand and water;

b salt from a salt solution.

7 Look at the label found on a bottle of mineral water.

a Name <u>one</u> substance dissolved in the mineral water.

b Describe how you could prove that the mineral water contains dissolved substances.

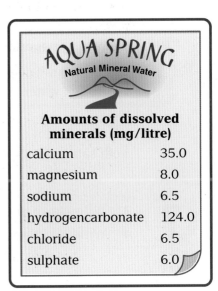

AQUA SPRING

Natural Mineral Water

Amounts of dissolved minerals (mg/litre)

calcium	35.0
magnesium	8.0
sodium	6.5
hydrogencarbonate	124.0
chloride	6.5
sulphate	6.0

8 We use many different separation techniques in cooking. Describe <u>three</u> situations in cooking that use different separation techniques.

7H.2 Salt of the Earth

The chemical name for salt is **sodium chloride**. Sodium chloride is often called 'common salt'. There are two main places where people find salt:

- There is a type of rock that contains a large amount of salt. This is called <u>rock salt</u>.

- There is salt in sea water.

Different countries use different methods to get common salt.

Crushed rock salt.

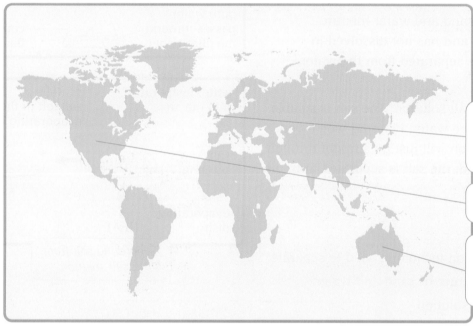

In the UK, water is pumped into the rock salt. The salt dissolves and the salt solution is pumped to the surface.

In the USA, rock salt is mined by cutting, drilling and blasting.

In Australia, sea water is collected. Sunlight is used to evaporate the water until salt crystals form.

?

1   What is the chemical name for 'common salt'?
2   In Australia, salt is obtained by the crystallisation of sea water. Why isn't this method used in the UK?

We spend a lot of money extracting salt. This is because both salt and rock salt have a variety of uses.

?

3   Write down <u>one</u> use of rock salt.
4   Write down <u>one</u> use of sodium chloride.

5   Sodium chloride is an important part of our diet. Try to find out why our bodies need sodium chloride.

chlorine
used to make bleach

sodium carbonate
used to make glass

salt "sodium chloride"

rock salt
spread on roads in winter to melt snow and ice

sodium hydroxide
used to make soap and detergents

Some of the uses of salt.

7H.3 The mystery of the disappearing solute!

When we dissolve salt in water, we make a colourless solution. Although the salt seems to 'vanish', it is still there. The salt reappears when the water is evaporated away. We need to explain how the salt can seem to 'vanish'.

Balanced solutions

The biggest clue to what happens to the salt when we make a solution comes from weighing. We can weigh the salt and water separately before making a solution. We can then weigh the solution that we have made.

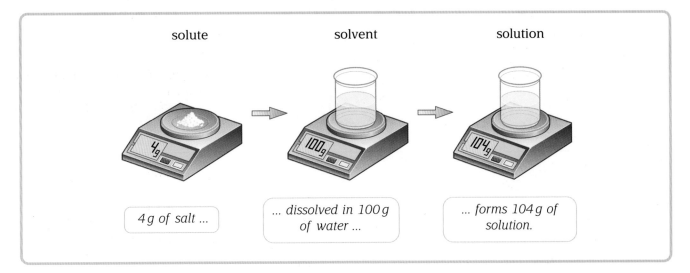

solute   solvent   solution

4 g of salt ...

... dissolved in 100 g of water ...

... forms 104 g of solution.

This is true for every solution: the mass of a solution always equals the total mass of the solute and the solvent. We can write this as an equation:

mass of solute + mass of solvent = mass of solution

This tells us that when a solute dissolves it hasn't really 'vanished'. It is part of the solution, so no mass is lost. This is called <u>conservation of mass</u>.

1   What mass of salt solution is made from 7 g of salt and 40 g of water?

2   What mass of salt must be added to 100 g of water to make a salt solution with a mass of 105 g?

A closer look at solutions

To explain why the solute seems to 'vanish' when we make a solution, we need to use the idea of **particles**.

When a solute dissolves it breaks apart into its individual particles. The solute and solvent particles mix together and become totally mixed up. That's why a solution is a mixture! As the solute and solvent particles become mixed up, no matter is lost. The overall mass stays the same.

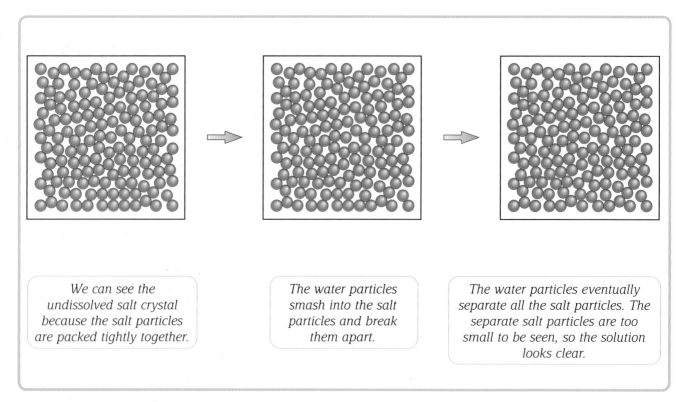

We can see the undissolved salt crystal because the salt particles are packed tightly together.

The water particles smash into the salt particles and break them apart.

The water particles eventually separate all the salt particles. The separate salt particles are too small to be seen, so the solution looks clear.

3 How do the solvent particles break up the solute?

4 Describe how the solute and solvent particles are arranged in a solution.

5 10 g of salt is dissolved in 100 g of water. Use the idea of particles to explain why the mass of the salt solution is 110 g.

6 Why is it not possible to get the salt out of a salt solution using filtration? You need to think about:

- how the salt and water particles are arranged in a solution;
- the size of the salt and water particles and the size of the 'holes' in filter paper.

7H.4 Separating solvents from solutes

We have already seen how to get the solute back from a solution. When we heat a salt solution, the water evaporates and leaves the salt behind. We now need to find a way to collect the water.

The separation and collection of water from a solution is important if we want to be able to purify water. It is often important in chemistry experiments to use extremely pure water that contains no dissolved impurities. This pure water is called <u>distilled water</u>. The name 'distilled water' gives us a big clue to how the water has been purified.

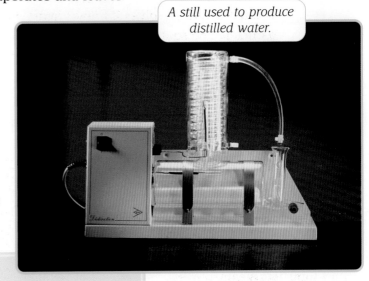

A still used to produce distilled water.

1 What is the name of the pure water used in some chemistry experiments?

2 Why is it important sometimes to use pure water?

Getting the solvent back – distillation

You may have noticed that bathroom mirrors steam up when you have a hot bath. The hot steam from the bath hits the cold mirror. The cold mirror cools the steam back into water. This is called **condensation**.

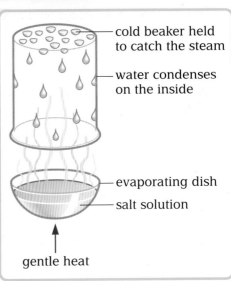

Everyday condensation.

3 Why does the steam change into water when it hits the mirror?

4 What is the process called when steam changes back into water?

It is the idea that steam changes back into water when the steam hits a cold surface that helps us separate water from a salt solution.

When a salt solution is heated up the water evaporates as steam. The water changes state from a liquid to a gas. The steam can be condensed back into pure water by cooling it down. The steam changes state from a gas back into a liquid. All we need now is a way to collect the water.

cold beaker held to catch the steam

water condenses on the inside

evaporating dish

salt solution

gentle heat

5 Describe the changes of state that occur during:

   a evaporation;

   b condensation.

The water is collected using a **condenser**. This whole process is called **distillation**.

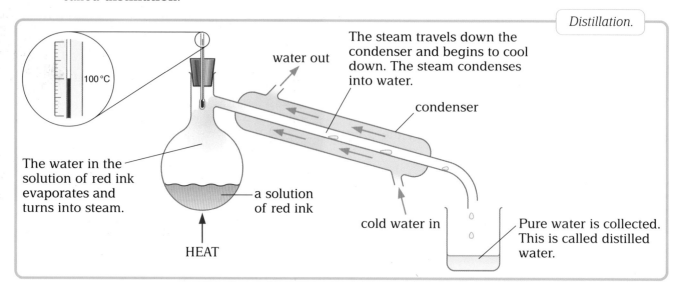

Distillation.

The steam travels down the condenser and begins to cool down. The steam condenses into water.

condenser

water out

The water in the solution of red ink evaporates and turns into steam.

a solution of red ink

cold water in

Pure water is collected. This is called distilled water.

HEAT

100 °C

Distillation is the process in which the evaporation of a liquid is followed by its condensation:

- evaporation – the liquid solvent changes to a gas as it is heated up;

- condensation – the gas changes back into a liquid as it is cooled down.

During distillation the solute doesn't evaporate, so the solute is left behind in the flask.

6 What is the temperature reading on the thermometer?

7 Explain why the thermometer shows this temperature.

8 The condenser is named after a German scientist who believed in using practical work to teach chemistry. Try to find out the name of this scientist and any other contributions he made to chemistry.

7H.5 Chromatography

Some solutions contain a mixture of different solutes. The technique used to separate a mixture of two or more solutes is called **chromatography**.

This diagram shows one method you can use to do chromatography in a school laboratory.

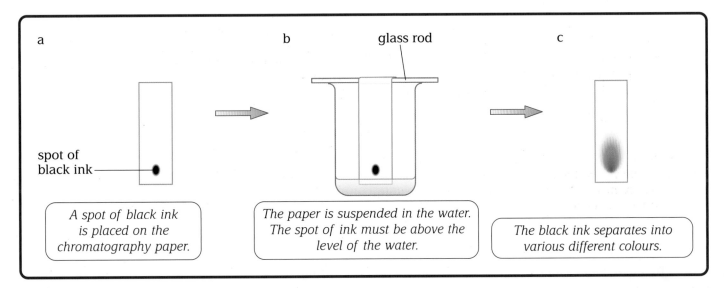

a

spot of black ink —

A spot of black ink is placed on the chromatography paper.

b   glass rod

The paper is suspended in the water. The spot of ink must be above the level of the water.

c

The black ink separates into various different colours.

1 Black ink is a mixture. Look at these diagrams. Which colours of ink are mixed to make the black ink?

2 What is this method of separation called?

3 Why mustn't the spot of black ink be placed in the water?

Water is a solvent for the ink. As the water is soaked up by the filter paper the water dissolves the ink. As the water spreads out it carries the ink with it. The ink particles are **attracted** to the water particles. The water particles move the particles of ink by giving them 'piggyback rides'.

The more firmly an ink particle attaches itself to a water particle the further it will be carried in a given amount of time.

4 What is the result of chromatography called?

*The piece of chromatography paper shows how the parts of the mixture have been separated. The piece of paper is called a **chromatogram**.*

The black ink is a mixture of yellow, red, brown and blue inks. The yellow ink has been carried the furthest. So, the yellow ink is the most soluble in water. The blue ink has been carried the least. So the blue ink is the least soluble in water.

Chromatography only works if the test mixture is soluble in the solvent. For example, not all paints are soluble in water. So, we need to use a different solvent, such as white spirit, that will dissolve the paint.

5 A sample of blue paint doesn't dissolve in water. How would you carry out chromatography on this paint?

Making use of chromatography

One possible use of chromatography is to study food dyes. Some foods are coloured using a mixture of food dyes. You may want to find out which food dyes have been used in a particular food if you are allergic to one food dye.

We can use chromatography to find out how many different food dyes are used to make the coloured coatings on chocolate sweets.

This chromatogram shows that the blue and yellow food colourings are pure, but the brown food colouring is a mixture of red, yellow and blue.

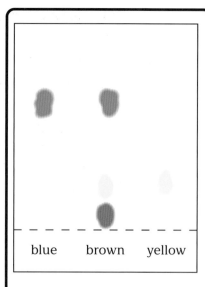

blue   brown   yellow

Chromatography results for blue, brown and yellow food colourings.

6 How many different dyes does Food Colouring 1 contain?

7 Name the dyes found in Food Colouring 2.

8 Which dye is the most soluble?

9 You have an allergic reaction to Food Colouring 2 but not Food Colouring 1. Which food dye are you allergic to?

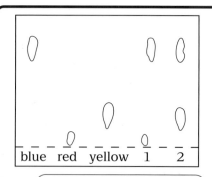

blue   red   yellow   1   2

Chromatography results for blue, red and yellow food dyes and two different food colourings.

More uses of chromatography

Scientists use chromatography to help them in a wide range of situations. These include:

- biology, for example finding out which pigments are contained in leaves;
- forensic science, for example comparing the blood of a suspect with blood found at the scene of a crime;
- medicine, for example testing urine to identify traces of substances in it to check a patient's health.

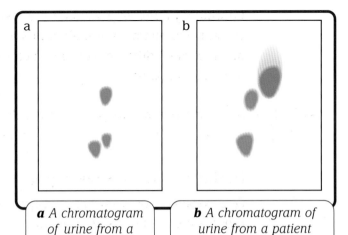

a A chromatogram of urine from a healthy person.

b A chromatogram of urine from a patient suffering from phenylketonuria.

10 Two cars were involved in an accident. One driver drove off without stopping. However, some red paint was left behind on the other car. The police have three suspects, each owning red cars. Describe how they could use chromatography to prove which red car was involved in the accident.

7H.6 Solubility

If we keep adding salt to water at room temperature there comes a point when no more salt will dissolve. However hard we try, there is a limit to the amount of solid that dissolves in a particular volume of water. A solution where no more solid will dissolve is called a **saturated solution**.

1 What happens to salt that is added to a saturated solution?

2 How can you tell that a salt solution is saturated?

Solubility

We already know that some solids are soluble in water whilst others are insoluble. In fact, different solids are soluble in different amounts. For example, sodium chloride is very soluble and dissolves easily in water, but lead chloride is only slightly soluble and is quite hard to dissolve in water.

Solubility is a measure of how soluble something is. The higher its solubility the more soluble it is.

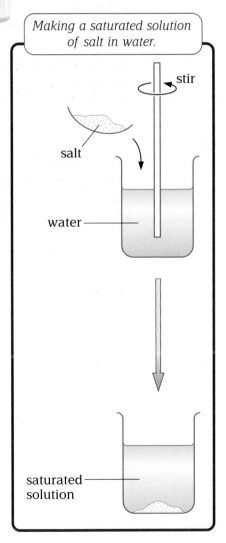

Making a saturated solution of salt in water.

stir

salt

water

saturated solution

To compare the solubility of different solutes we need to make the comparison fair. To do this we measure the maximum mass of a solute that will dissolve in 100 g of the solvent. In effect, what we are doing is starting with 100 g of a solvent and measuring how much solute we can dissolve until we make a saturated solution.

Substance	Solubility in grams per 100 g of water
calcium chloride	74
copper sulphate	21
potassium chlorate	7
potassium nitrate	300
sand	0
sodium chloride	36

3 What do we call the measure of how soluble something is?

4 Look at the table. Which substance is the most soluble in water?

5 Which substance is insoluble in water? Explain your answer.

Changing the solvent

Imagine you have spilt some oil on your shirt. You have to buy a special stain remover to remove the oil. The stain remover does this because it contains a solvent that dissolves the oil.

If we want to dissolve a solid we have to select the solvent very carefully. This means that we must name the solvent when solubility is stated. For example, sodium chloride has a solubility of 36 g in 100 g of water.

Different stains need different stain removers.

6 Name <u>one</u> substance that doesn't dissolve in water.

7 Why must the solvent be named when solubility is stated?

8 Different stain removers are designed to remove different stains. How can they do this?

Temperature and solubility

You may have noticed that sugar is easy to dissolve in a cup of hot tea, but not so easy to dissolve if the tea is cooler.

For many solutes their solubility increases as the temperature increases. This means that more solute will dissolve in a warm solvent than in a cold solvent. It is important that the temperature is given when solubility is stated. For example, sodium chloride has a solubility of 36 g in 100 g of water <u>at 20 °C</u>.

When we compare the solubility of different solutes, we often need to do so for a range of temperatures.

A good way of showing how solubility changes as the temperature changes is to plot the data as a graph.

The graph here shows that the solubility of all three solids increases as the temperature increases. The curves can be used to work out the solubility of any of the solids at any temperature. For example, we can see that the solubility of copper sulphate in 100 g of water at 80 °C is 55 g. Having the three curves on the same graph also lets us compare the solubility of the three solids.

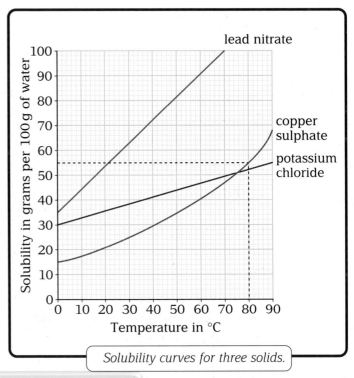

Solubility curves for three solids.

9   What happens to the solubility of all three solids as the temperature increases?

10 What is the solubility of lead nitrate at 60 °C?

11 Which solid is the most soluble at 10 °C?

12 At what temperature are the solubilities of potassium chloride and copper sulphate the same?

13 The solubility of which solid is most affected by temperature?

14 Rob made a cup of coffee using coffee granules in a mug of hot water. Unfortunately, Rob forgot about the coffee. The next day he found that there was solid coffee in the bottom of the mug. Use the ideas of solubility and saturated solutions to explain this.

You should now understand the key words and key ideas shown below.

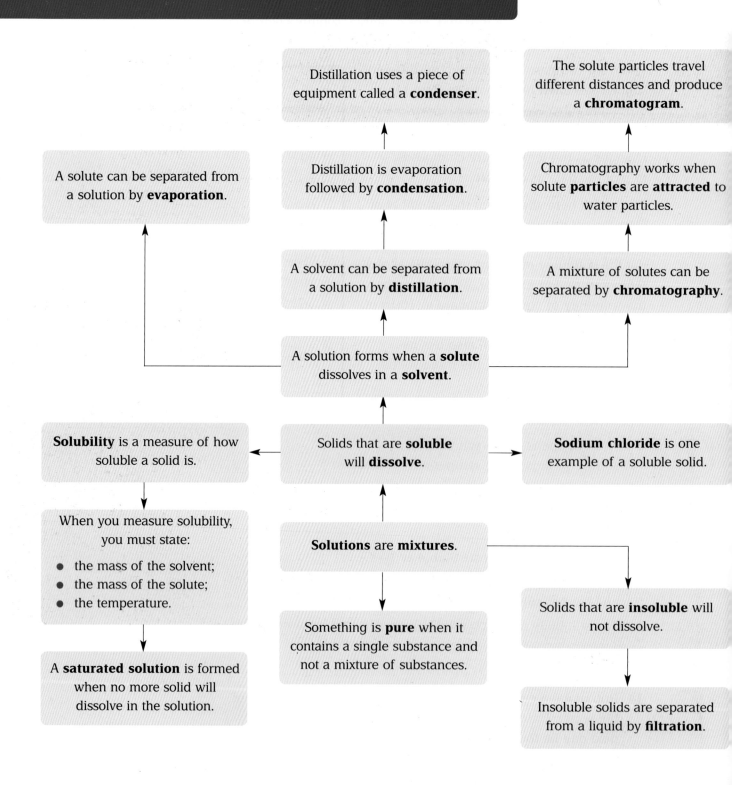

Distillation uses a piece of equipment called a **condenser**.

The solute particles travel different distances and produce a **chromatogram**.

A solute can be separated from a solution by **evaporation**.

Distillation is evaporation followed by **condensation**.

Chromatography works when solute **particles** are **attracted** to water particles.

A solvent can be separated from a solution by **distillation**.

A mixture of solutes can be separated by **chromatography**.

A solution forms when a **solute** dissolves in a **solvent**.

Solubility is a measure of how soluble a solid is.

Solids that are **soluble** will **dissolve**.

Sodium chloride is one example of a soluble solid.

When you measure solubility, you must state:

- the mass of the solvent;
- the mass of the solute;
- the temperature.

Solutions are **mixtures**.

Solids that are **insoluble** will not dissolve.

A **saturated solution** is formed when no more solid will dissolve in the solution.

Something is **pure** when it contains a single substance and not a mixture of substances.

Insoluble solids are separated from a liquid by **filtration**.

Atoms and elements

In this unit we shall be learning about atoms and elements, and how atoms can join together to make compounds.

KEY WORDS
material
element
atom
particle
symbol
molecule
compound
formula

8E.1 Materials

Early ideas about elements

The photograph shows a **material**. You need to remember that a <u>material</u> is not the same as an <u>object</u>. Think about an ordinary ruler. The ruler is an object, and it is made out of plastic, which is a material.

We group materials in many different ways:

- natural and made;
- metals and non-metals;
- ceramics;
- fibres and plastics.

The Ancient Greeks thought that all materials were made up of four basic materials – Earth, Fire, Air and Water. They called them the four 'Elements'. For example, liquids such as wine or oil were thought to be mostly 'Water', and solids such as bread or iron were thought to be mostly 'Earth'.

Now we know that Earth, Fire, Air and Water are not elements at all, and that there are many more than just four elements. Our idea of what an element is has changed completely.

Wood is the <u>material</u> which makes up this pepper mill. The pepper mill is an <u>object</u>. Wood is a natural material.

1 What were the four 'Elements', according to the Ancient Greeks?

Elements today

Today we know that there are about 100 **elements**, and that there is something very special about them. Every element is a pure substance, and no element can be made out of anything else.

When you look at some materials with a microscope you can <u>see</u> that they are made up of different things. For example, concrete contains pieces of sand and different coloured crystals. Materials which contain several different things cannot be elements, so it is easy to see that concrete is not an element. Sometimes it is not so easy to tell. For example, glass, rubber and polythene are not elements. You just can't see that they contain different things.

Diamond is made of carbon only. Carbon and gold are elements.

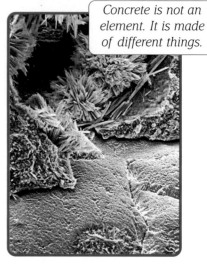
Concrete is not an element. It is made of different things.

2 What is so special about elements?

3 How can you be certain that wood is not an element?

Arab, and then European scientists, called alchemists continued where the Greeks left off. They studied and tried to change materials. By the 18ᵗʰ century, scientists realised that some of the new materials they discovered, such as phosphorus, hydrogen and oxygen, were themselves elements.

These scientists recognised that every element was a pure substance. They were thinking of elements in the same way as we think of them today. One aim of many of the alchemists was to turn lead into gold. Eighteenth-century scientists started to understand that no element could be made out of anything else.

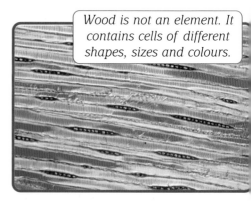
Wood is not an element. It contains cells of different shapes, sizes and colours.

> Remember: every element is a pure substance, and no element can be made out of anything else.

Now we know that all the countless different materials in the world are made from the 100 or so elements. We think of elements as the 'building blocks' of nature from which everything is made, including us.

4 There are just over 100 different elements. Find out the names of <u>10</u> elements you have not heard of before.

8E.2 What the elements are like

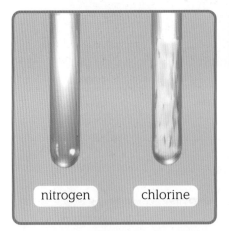
nitrogen   chlorine

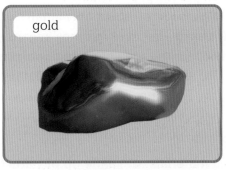
gold

carbon

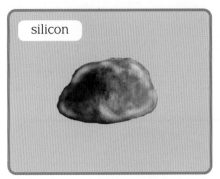
silicon

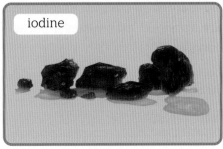
iodine

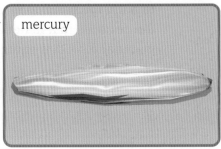
mercury

sodium

sulphur

All these are elements.

There are about 100 different elements. Some elements, such as gold and copper, have been known since prehistoric times. Other elements, such as radium, have only been known for about 100 years. Scientists are quite sure now that they have discovered all the <u>natural</u> elements. Scientists think it may be possible to make more new elements artificially.

Unlike materials such as wood, oil and soil, elements cannot be made up from anything else. This is because elements contain just one thing – themselves. All the other materials in the world are made from these 100 or so elements.

1   About how many elements are there?

Introducing atoms

Over 2000 years ago a Greek philosopher called Democritus suggested that everything was made of uncuttably small **particles**, which he called '**atoms**' (in Greek 'atomos' means 'uncuttable'). Many centuries later the idea became popular again, and in the nineteenth century scientists such as John Dalton began to find evidence for the existence of atoms. Because atoms are so small – too small to see even with a microscope – it was not easy to convince everybody that they existed.

Now scientists think that all materials are made up of particles that are too small to see. You learned in Unit 7G that it is the way the particles in a material are arranged that makes a particular material a solid, a liquid or a gas.

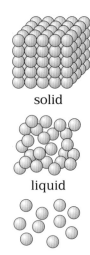

solid

liquid

gas

The arrangement of particles in solids, liquids and gases.

2 How are the particles arranged in a gas?

3 What does the word 'atom' mean?

Evidence for the existence of particles is all around us, and without the idea of particles there would be an endless number of things we could not explain. If you polish a piece of aluminium with a cloth you can smell the metal. This is because particles of aluminium (aluminium atoms) have gone into the air – and up your nose!

Atoms are one type of particle. We now know that every element has its own special kind of atom. There are oxygen atoms, iron atoms, carbon atoms, aluminium atoms, and so on. Each kind of atom is different from other kinds in its size and its properties.

You can smell the aluminium – this is evidence for the existence of aluminium atoms.

4 How does your nose provide evidence that particles exist?

We usually picture atoms as being tiny spheres, like marbles or ball-bearings. Imagine a large number of Lego pieces, all of the same colour, stuck together to make a huge Lego lump. It's a bit like this with atoms – you can arrange them to make different shapes. This is how we can get crystals of different shapes.

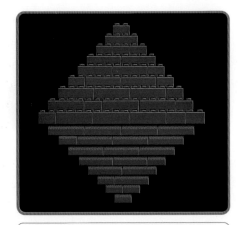

This large 'lump' of Lego is made from lots of identical small Lego pieces stuck together.

These iodine crystals are made from millions of iodine atoms held together.

Sodium chloride crystals are made up of sodium particles and chloride particles held together.

5 What type of atoms would you find in a lump of the element iron?

We now have a good idea of the size of atoms and molecules. Hydrogen atoms, the smallest of all, are about $0.0000001\,mm$ across.

6 About how big are the atoms that make up hydrogen?

7 Do you think carbon dioxide is an element?
Explain your answer.

Tables of elements

The table shows some of the common elements. It shows the chemical symbol for each element and some other useful information.

Name	Symbol	Metal or non-metal	Solid, liquid or gas at 20 °C	Colour	Year discovered
bromine	Br	non-metal	liquid	brown	1826
calcium	Ca	metal	solid	grey	1808
carbon	C	non-metal	solid	black	ancient
chlorine	Cl	non-metal	gas	green	1810
cobalt	Co	metal	solid	grey	1739
copper	Cu	metal	solid	pink	ancient
gold	Au	metal	solid	gold	ancient
helium	He	non-metal	gas	colourless	1868
hydrogen	H	non-metal	gas	colourless	1783
iron	Fe	metal	solid	grey	ancient
magnesium	Mg	metal	solid	grey	1808
mercury	Hg	metal	liquid	silver	ancient
nitrogen	N	non-metal	gas	colourless	1772
oxygen	O	non-metal	gas	colourless	1774
phosphorus	P	non-metal	solid	white	1669
silver	Ag	metal	solid	silver	ancient
sulphur	S	non-metal	solid	yellow	ancient

People have known about some elements, such as copper, silver and gold, for a long time. These elements already had common, everyday names in most languages. As scientists discovered new elements, they had to give them names. They chose the names for the new elements with great care and often tried to make their names fit what they were like. For example, the name 'chlorine' comes from a Greek word 'chloros' meaning green, and 'oxygen' means 'acid-maker'.

Every element has a **symbol** as well as a name. Some symbols are single letters, like O for oxygen; others have two letters, as in Au for gold. When there are two letters, the first is always a capital letter and the second is always a small letter. This is very important: Cu means copper but CU means carbon with uranium – something very different!

> The Periodic Table contains information about all the elements. You may have one in your science laboratory.

Scientists use the symbol to represent one atom of an element, and use a small number below the line if there is more than one atom. So, Fe means 'one atom of iron' and O_2 means 'two atoms of oxygen'.

8 What does Cl_2 mean?

9 What is the difference between CO and Co?

10 Which of the following are <u>not</u> atoms?

    a O_2 **b** H_2 **c** He

    d CO_2 **e** C

11 Find out about the discovery of helium and where its name comes from.

Introducing molecules

Atoms are particles and so are **molecules**. Molecules are groups of atoms stuck together in twos, threes, and so on; some molecules contain hundreds of atoms.

Sometimes a molecule contains two atoms that are the same. An example is an oxygen molecule, which is shown as O_2. However, there may be many different kinds of atom combined in a molecule. For example, carbon dioxide contains two different kinds of atoms and ammonium chloride contains three different kinds of atoms (the 'ammonium' bit contains hydrogen and nitrogen).

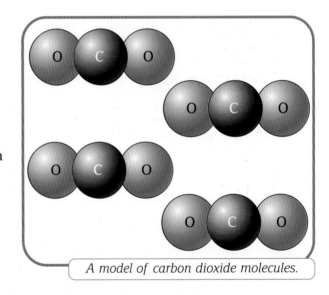

A model of carbon dioxide molecules.

12 What is the minimum number of atoms in a molecule?

8E.3 How we get all the other materials

There are two types of changes: <u>physical changes</u> and <u>chemical changes</u>.

Physical changes are things like melting and freezing, expanding and contracting. It is usually quite easy to reverse a physical change.

Just put the water back in the freezer to reverse this physical change.

Chemical changes are very different. The important difference is that it is usually very difficult, and sometimes impossible, to reverse a chemical change. This is because chemical changes actually make <u>new</u> materials, and do not just change the same material into a different form.

Burning is an example of an <u>irreversible</u> change you will already have met. Burning is only one example; here are some more:

- digesting food;
- leaves rotting away;
- iron rusting;
- cooking food;
- concrete setting.

Burning is an irreversible chemical change.

1   Give <u>one</u> example of a physical change and <u>one</u> example of a chemical change.

2   Looking at the remains of a bonfire gives a strong clue that burning is a chemical change. What is this clue?

Making new materials

We use chemical changes to get thousands of different materials from a limited number of starting materials. Sometimes materials can be put together to make new materials:

Making soap, the Roman way.

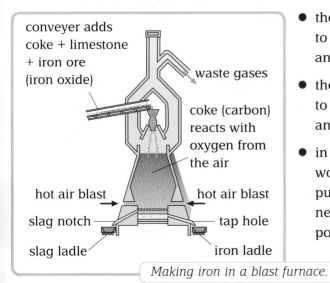

conveyer adds coke + limestone + iron ore (iron oxide)

waste gases

coke (carbon) reacts with oxygen from the air

hot air blast

hot air blast

slag notch

tap hole

slag ladle

iron ladle

Making iron in a blast furnace.

- the Romans knew how to make soap from soda and fat;

- the Romans knew how to make glass from soda and sand;

- in a modern chemical works, oil products are put together to make new materials such as polystyrene.

Polystyrene is made from oil.

When elements are combined together they form **compounds**. In most cases, what a compound is like does not seem to give any clue about the elements it contains. For example:

- sodium is a very reactive silvery metal;

- chlorine is a poisonous green gas.

Yet, sodium combines with chlorine to form sodium chloride, which is a harmless white solid known as common salt. Remember that we can think of a piece of an element as a huge Lego lump made up of millions of exactly the same type of brick. In the same way, we can think of compounds as being made up from two, or three, or more different types of brick. There will be a basic pattern, repeated again and again.

This model could represent chalk. The basic pattern, 1 red + 3 white + 1 yellow, represents the basic structure of the compound.

3   Water is a compound made from the elements hydrogen and oxygen. How is water different from the elements it contains?

4   What is the smallest number of different kinds of element a compound can contain?

5   Find out how sodium and chloride particles are arranged in a crystal of sodium chloride. Include a diagram in your answer.

8E.4 Representing the changes

Each compound is known by its **formula** and its name. For example, <u>carbon dioxide</u> is a compound. Each molecule of carbon dioxide contains one atom of carbon and two atoms of oxygen. We can write the formula of carbon dioxide as CO_2.

carbon dioxide

> The plural of 'formula' is 'formulae'.

Chemical names of compounds are a description of what is in them. For example, copper oxide contains copper and oxygen. We use the symbols of these elements to write the formula, so the formula of copper oxide is CuO.

Sometimes, as with carbon dioxide, the formula has small numbers below the line to tell you the ratio of each element present. CO_2 means that carbon dioxide has one atom of carbon for every two atoms of oxygen.

Every compound has a 'proper' chemical name, even if it already has an 'everyday' name. For example, common salt is sodium chloride and chalk is calcium carbonate.

The ending to the name is important. Names that end in 'ide' have two elements present. Names that end in 'ate' have three elements present including oxygen. So, calcium carbonate is made up of calcium, carbon and oxygen.

'Pass the sodium chloride please.'

Calcium carbonate.

1 What is the difference between the everyday name for a compound and its chemical name?

2 What elements do you think these compounds contain?

   a copper chloride

   b zinc sulphide

   c nitrogen oxide

3 These are the formulae of real compounds. Work out the name for each of them.

   a CaO

   b MgS

   c HCl

More formulae and equations

Compounds may have different names in different languages, but their formulae are always the same. So a scientist, in any country, can recognise a compound by its formula.

Scientists can work out the formula for water by splitting water into hydrogen and oxygen. This shows that water contains twice as much hydrogen as oxygen. So, the formula of water is H_2O.

We represent chemical reactions with <u>chemical equations</u>. We write them using the names (a word equation), using formulae (a symbol equation), or both!

Water is H_2O everywhere in the world.

$$C \quad + \quad O_2 \quad \rightarrow \quad CO_2$$

carbon   oxygen   carbon dioxide

We can also add information about the chemicals we start with, the <u>reactants</u>, and the chemicals we make, the <u>products</u>.

$$2Mg \quad + \quad O_2 \quad \rightarrow \quad 2MgO$$

magnesium   oxygen   magnesium oxide

<u>reactants</u>   <u>product</u>

In the two equations above, O_2 represents a <u>molecule</u> of oxygen gas. An oxygen molecule is made up of two oxygen atoms joined together. This sort of molecule is called a diatomic molecule. Many of the common gases, including hydrogen, nitrogen and chlorine, have molecules of this kind.

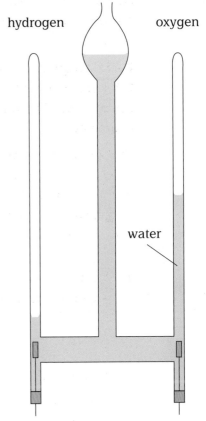

hydrogen   oxygen

water

negative   positive
electrode   electrode

One way of splitting up water is by using electricity – this process is called electrolysis. A Hofmann voltameter is used for the electrolysis of water. Half as much oxygen is produced as hydrogen.

4   What is a diatomic molecule?

5   Write a word equation to show copper reacting with sulphur to make copper sulphide.

6   Calcium reacts with oxygen. Write a word equation for this.

7   Look at the equation for the reaction between magnesium and oxygen. Explain why we need two atoms of Mg and why we make two lots of MgO as the product.

You should now understand the key words and key ideas shown below.

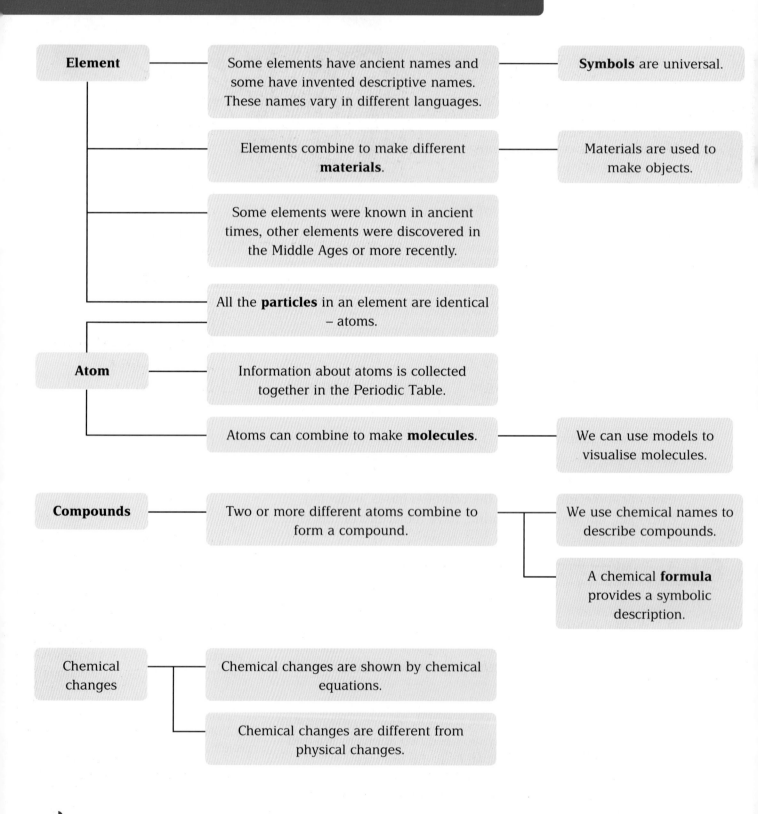

Element

Some elements have ancient names and some have invented descriptive names. These names vary in different languages.

Symbols are universal.

Elements combine to make different **materials**.

Materials are used to make objects.

Some elements were known in ancient times, other elements were discovered in the Middle Ages or more recently.

All the **particles** in an element are identical – atoms.

Atom

Information about atoms is collected together in the Periodic Table.

Atoms can combine to make **molecules**.

We can use models to visualise molecules.

Compounds

Two or more different atoms combine to form a compound.

We use chemical names to describe compounds.

A chemical **formula** provides a symbolic description.

Chemical changes

Chemical changes are shown by chemical equations.

Chemical changes are different from physical changes.

Compounds and mixtures

In this unit we shall be looking at elements and compounds in more detail. We shall also look at mixtures and see how they differ from both pure elements and compounds. In particular, we shall look at an important mixture that is all around us – the air!

KEY WORDS
atoms
elements
compounds
react
mixture
oxygen
nitrogen
argon
carbon dioxide
water vapour
liquefied
fractional distillation
melting point
boiling point

8F.1 Elements and compounds

In Unit 8E, you learnt that all substances are made up of small particles called **atoms**. Some pure substances are made up of only one type of atom. These pure substances cannot be broken down into anything simpler by a chemical reaction. We call these substances **elements**.

There are only 92 different elements found naturally on Earth. Atoms of these elements join together and make millions of different substances. Substances formed from two or more elements chemically joined together are called **compounds**.

We can think of elements and compounds like we think of letters and words. There are only 26 letters in the alphabet but we can use them to make all the words in a dictionary.

? 1 Read the passage about noble gases, then:

  a count the number of different words used;

  b find out how many different letters are used;

  c write down the words that contain only one letter;

  d find the word that has the greatest number of different letters.

 2 Why did the inert gases go undetected for centuries?

There are inert gases in the air we breathe. They have strange Greek names which mean "the New", "the Hidden", "the Inactive" and "the Alien". They are so satisfied with their condition that they do not join with any other element. Only forty years ago did a chemist finally succeed in forcing the Alien (xenon) to combine briefly with the element fluorine.

Now, we often call inert gases the noble gases.

Many elements are well-known substances. Oxygen, iron and copper are examples. However, some elements are very rare and you do not see them very often. Samarium is an example.

3 Look at the pictures of one use of each of four elements. Which element:

   a is a shiny metal used to build bridges?

   b is a gas in the air, that you can't do without?

   c is a gas used in airships?

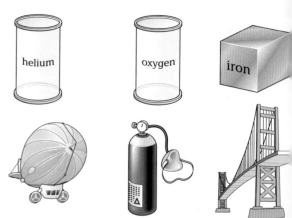

helium   oxygen   iron

We cannot see atoms because they are very small. However, we can represent what an element or compound looks like by using models. Models will show which atoms are found in the substance.

4 In the particle diagram, which substances are elements and which substances are compounds?

We can describe each of these substances using a chemical formula. A chemical formula tells you how many atoms of each element there are in the smallest particle of the substance.

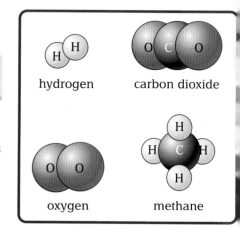

hydrogen   carbon dioxide

oxygen   methane

5 How many atoms does one particle of water contain?

6 Work out the formula for each substance shown in the particle diagram.

7 Look at the formulae given on the bottles. For each formula work out:

   a how many atoms it contains;

   b how many different elements are present.

8 The labels for these compounds have fallen off the bottles. Match the names of the compounds to the correct bottles.

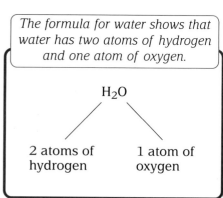

The formula for water shows that water has two atoms of hydrogen and one atom of oxygen.

$$H_2O$$

2 atoms of hydrogen   1 atom of oxygen

H_2SO_4 $CaCO_3$ MgO $CuSO_4$

calcium carbonate   sulphuric acid   copper sulphate   magnesium oxide

8F.2 Looking at compounds

<u>Sodium chloride</u> is a compound made from the elements <u>sodium</u> and <u>chlorine</u>.

When these two elements meet, they **react** violently to produce white crystals of sodium chloride. It is a new substance made from two different elements, so it is a compound. We know that the reaction is a chemical reaction because salt is very different from both sodium and chlorine. Compounds are always different from the elements they are made from.

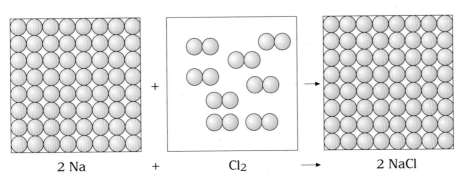

2 Na   +   Cl₂   ⟶   2 NaCl

This particle diagram shows the reaction between sodium and chlorine.

Sodium is a reactive metal that will react violently with water to produce hydrogen.

Chlorine is a pale green gas which is very poisonous.

1   What is the chemical symbol for sodium?

2   What is the chemical symbol for chlorine?

3   What is the chemical formula for sodium chloride?

We can describe what happens in this chemical reaction by writing a word equation. In a word equation the reactants are shown on the left-hand side of the arrow and the products are shown on the right-hand side of the arrow.

sodium + chlorine → sodium chloride
      reactants   product

Sodium chloride is the salt that we add to our food to give it a salty taste.

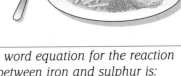

4   Look at the diagrams. Describe the appearance of iron and of sulphur.

5   Describe the differences between iron sulphide and:

a iron;

b sulphur.

The word equation for the reaction between iron and sulphur is:
iron + sulphur → iron sulphide

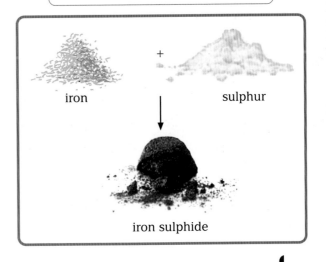

iron   +   sulphur

iron sulphide

8F.3 Compounds and some of their reactions

Some compounds are very reactive. However, some compounds are less reactive and will only react under certain conditions.

 1 Look at the pictures. Describe the evidence they give for chemical reactions.

In earlier units you saw many different types of reactions, including:

- reactions with oxygen. Words used to describe reactions with oxygen include 'burning', 'combustion', 'oxidation' and even respiration;

- neutralisation reactions. When an acid reacts with an alkali, the properties of the acid and alkali are cancelled out;

- precipitation reactions. In some reactions between two solutions, one of the products is insoluble and it settles as a solid called a <u>precipitate</u>;

- thermal decomposition reactions. Some compounds break down or <u>decompose</u> when you heat them. For example, calcium carbonate is broken down into the simpler substances calcium oxide and carbon dioxide when it is heated.

 2 Oxygen reacts with many different substances. Where does the oxygen come from for all these reactions?

 3 Find out how you can tell when:

a an acid has been neutralised;

b a gas is produced in a neutralisation reaction.

 4

| sodium carbonate solution | + | iron chloride solution | → | iron carbonate precipitate | + | sodium chloride solution |

For this reaction, explain how to separate the products.

 5 Write down the word equation for the thermal decomposition of calcium carbonate.

You know from Unit 7F that a chemical reaction may have taken place if:

- a gas is produced;

- a colour change happens;

- heat is produced;

- there is a change in mass;

- there is a change in appearance.

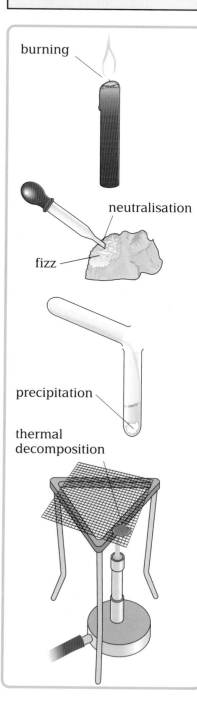

burning

neutralisation

fizz

precipitation

thermal decomposition

8F.4 What is a mixture?

A pure element is made up of identical particles, all of which are made up of the same type of atom.

A pure compound is made up of identical particles, but each particle contains two or more different types of atom chemically joined together.

However, many substances are mixtures. A **mixture** contains more than one substance and therefore it will contain more than one type of particle.

Look at the particle diagrams. Many substances are mixtures. There are different types of mixtures. You can have mixtures of:

- elements;
- compounds;
- elements and compounds.

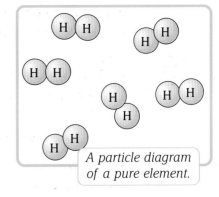

A particle diagram of a pure element.

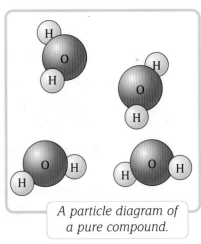

A particle diagram of a pure compound.

1 Look at the particle diagram of a mixture. How many different types of particles are there in this mixture?

2 Which of the particles present in the mixture are:

   a elements;

   b compounds?

3 Choosing your own elements and compounds, draw particle diagrams to show mixtures of:

   a two elements;

   b an element and a compound;

   c two compounds.

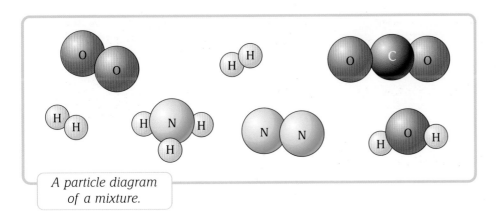

A particle diagram of a mixture.

You will come across many examples of mixtures. For example, mineral water is a mixture. Look at the label.

Typical analysis mg/1	
Calcium	60
Magnesium	15
Sodium	46
Potassium	2.2
Carbonate ($CaCO_3$)	145
Chloride	155
Sulphate	1
Nitrate	5
Fluoride	0.1
Total dissolved solids	**453**

4 How many different minerals are there in the mineral water?

5 Which mineral is:

a the most common?

b the least common?

6 Why can't you see the minerals in the water?

Sea water is also a mixture. It contains many different solids, called salts, dissolved in the water. There is an average of 40 g of salts dissolved in every kilogram of water from an ocean. But there are about 370 g of salts dissolved in every kilogram of water from the Dead Sea. The Dead Sea is the world's saltiest natural lake. It is an important mixture and is one of the greatest sources of minerals in the world. Over 43 billion tonnes of salts are thought to be dissolved in the Dead Sea, of which almost 2 billion tonnes are potassium chloride.

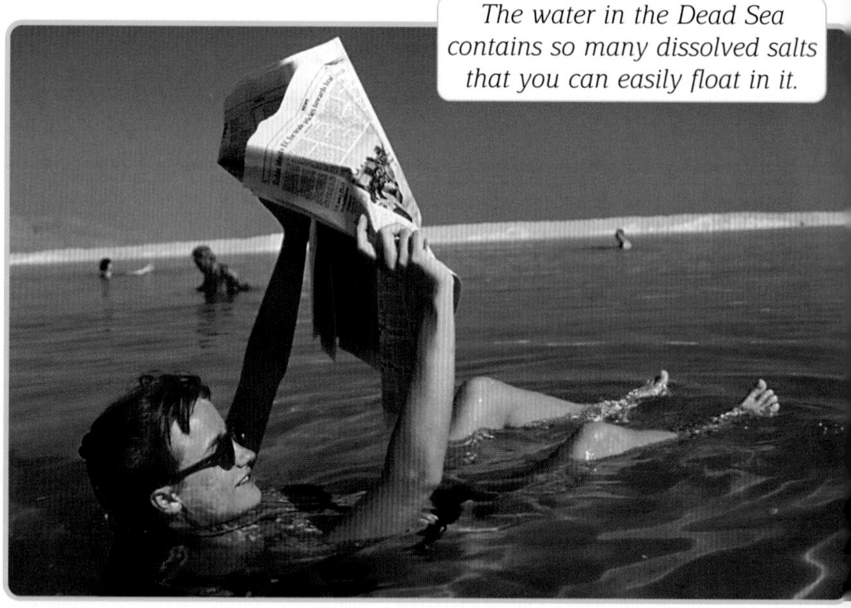

The water in the Dead Sea contains so many dissolved salts that you can easily float in it.

Salts in the Dead Sea

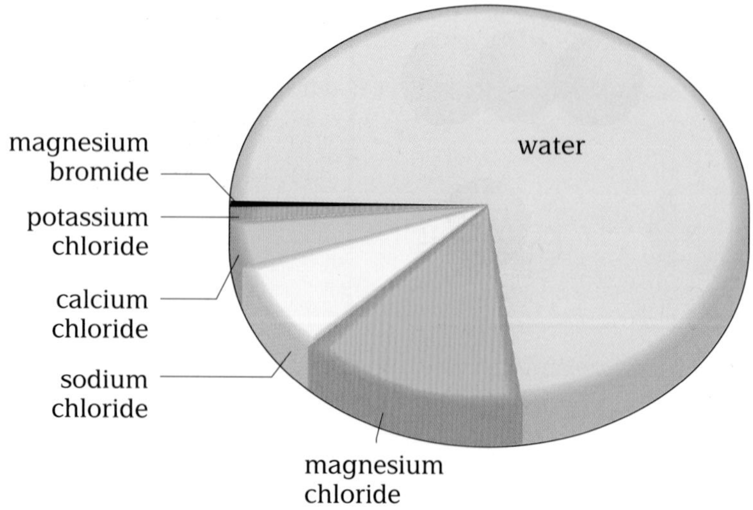

Mineral	**% mass**
magnesium chloride	14.5
sodium chloride	7.5
calcium chloride	3.8
potassium chloride	1.2
magnesium bromide	0.5
water	72.5

Mineral	**Amount** (billion tonnes)
magnesium chloride	22
sodium chloride	12
calcium chloride	6
potassium chloride	2
magnesium bromide	1

7 What is the most common compound in the Dead Sea mixture, after water?

8 What is the mass of calcium chloride in the Dead Sea?

The water going into the Dead Sea is not particularly salty. However, the local climate is extremely hot and dry, so the rate of evaporation of water is high. Water evaporates and leaves the salts behind. The Dead Sea is a bit like a huge evaporating basin.

9 a How many grams of salts are dissolved in every kilogram of water in the Dead Sea?

b How many times greater is this than the amount of salts dissolved in an ocean?

c How do all these salts get into the Dead Sea?

10 Why is the Dead Sea important for industry?

Air – a very special mixture

The air we breathe is a mixture of a number of very important gases.

Gas	Percentage in air
oxygen	21
nitrogen	78
argon (and other noble gases)	1
carbon dioxide	0.035
water	6 – 0.1

The gases in air.

11 Which gas makes up the biggest part of the mixture we call air?

12 What is the percentage of carbon dioxide in the air?

The most important gas in the air is the one that we all need to keep us alive – **oxygen**. We use oxygen to release the energy we need to keep our bodies working. We get our oxygen from the air and it is absorbed into our bloodstream through our lungs.

In hospital, patients with breathing or heart problems are sometimes given pure oxygen to breathe, rather than air. This makes it easier for them to absorb oxygen into their blood.

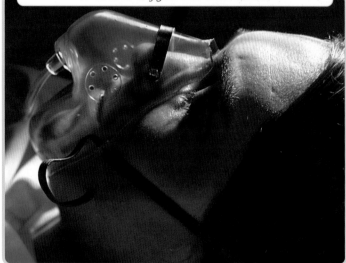

Oxygen is used in industry to produce important substances such as steel and nitric acid. Welders use oxygen to produce a very hot flame.

Nitrogen is an unreactive gas. This means we can use it to cool or store substances that react with oxygen, such as frozen food, chemicals and electronic equipment. We also use nitrogen to make the nitrate fertilisers that help crops grow.

There is a mixture of noble gases in the air but **argon** is the most common. Noble gases are very unreactive so they have little use in making new substances. Argon is the gas used inside light bulbs because it does not react with the tungsten filament in the bulbs.

Noble gases are used to produce bright lighting in advertising signs.

13 Write down:

    a <u>two</u> uses of oxygen;

    b <u>two</u> uses of nitrogen;

    c <u>one</u> use of noble gases.

We use **carbon dioxide** in some kinds of fire extinguishers, as it is very good at stopping things burning. Carbon dioxide is also the gas found in fizzy drinks. Also, we use solid carbon dioxide to store frozen food.

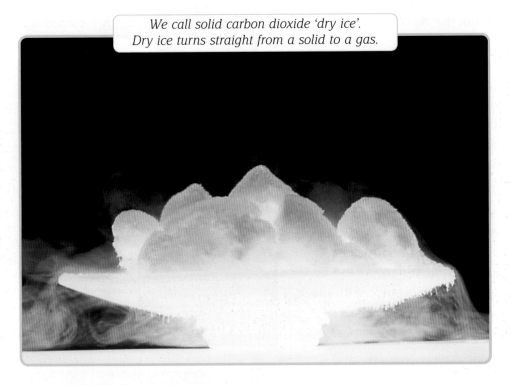

We call solid carbon dioxide 'dry ice'.
Dry ice turns straight from a solid to a gas.

The amount of **water vapour** in the air varies from day to day, depending on the weather. In some places the water vapour content can be as low as 0.1% but in a warm, humid climate it can be as high as 6%.

14 Draw a box filled with air showing all the different kinds of particles present.

Separating the gases in air

Air is a mixture of gases. Each gas in the mixture is a pure substance, so it has its own boiling point. In order to separate the gases present in air we must cool the mixture down. The first thing that happens is that water vapour condenses, and then solidifies. Then, as the air gets colder, carbon dioxide also becomes a solid.

15 At what temperature does water become a solid?

AIR

 16 Solid carbon dioxide and solid water would cause problems when the air mixture passed through pipes in the equipment used to separate air. Why is this?

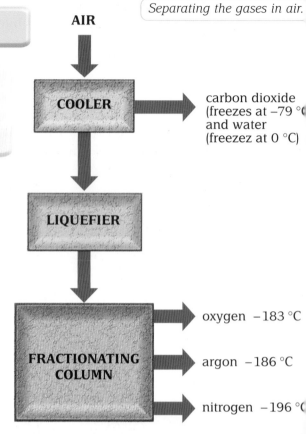

COOLER → carbon dioxide (freezes at −79 °C) and water (freezez at 0 °C)

LIQUEFIER

FRACTIONATING COLUMN → oxygen −183 °C

→ argon −186 °C

→ nitrogen −196 °C

The air is now dry and doesn't have any carbon dioxide in it. Next, the air is squashed to a high pressure, then allowed to expand quickly. This cools the air very quickly and it turns to a liquid. We say that the air has been **liquefied**.

Then the liquid air is allowed to warm up. It starts to boil. As the air warms up, the substance with the lowest boiling point boils first and turns into a gas. This gas is collected and stored. As the temperature rises slightly, the substance with the next lowest boiling point boils, and is collected and stored separately. So the gases are separated.

Over 95% of the oxygen used in industry and medicine is obtained from liquefied air.

This process of separating a mixture of liquids by heating them and collecting the gases as they boil off is called **fractional distillation**. We use a similar process to separate crude oil into simpler substances such as petrol and diesel. We also use distillation to separate the alcohol from water when we make drinks like whisky.

Liquid nitrogen.

 17 Which substance in air has the highest boiling point?

18 Which substance in air has the lowest boiling point?

 19 When liquefied air heats up, which is the first substance to become a gas?

20 Which substance in the liquefied air is the last to change back to a gas?

21 What is fractional distillation?

Boiling points of gases in air.

Gas	Boiling point
nitrogen	−196 °C
oxygen	−183 °C
argon	−186 °C
water	100 °C

 22 Write down <u>two</u> other uses of fractional distillation.

Mixtures and pure substances

- Iron is an element.
- Hydrogen is an element.
- Water is a compound.
- Methane is a compound.

But they are all pure substances.

 23 At room temperature, which of these substances are:

   a solids   **b** liquids   **c** gases

 24 How can you turn methane into a liquid?

If you cool water down, it eventually becomes a solid when the temperature is 0 °C. We call this solid <u>ice</u>. All pure substances, whether they are elements or compounds, have a fixed **melting point**.

If you heat water up it will eventually start to boil. This happens at a fixed boiling point of 100 °C. All elements and compounds have a fixed **boiling point.**

 25 What is the fixed melting point of ice?

     26 What is the fixed boiling point of water?

We can use the melting point or boiling point to tell us if the substance is pure. If we add salt to water the mixture doesn't boil at 100 °C, but at about 106 °C. Also, the mixture doesn't melt at 0 °C, but at about –6 °C. It depends on how much salt we add.

 27 We put salt on roads in winter when a frost is forecast. Why does salt help keep the roads clear of ice?

Mixtures are not pure substances, so they do not have fixed melting points or boiling points. A mixture will melt or boil over a range of temperatures. The exact range will depend on what is in the mixture. We add antifreeze to the water in a car's cooling system to make sure that it does not freeze if the temperature goes below 0 °C.

 28 Why is it bad for the engine when its cooling water freezes?

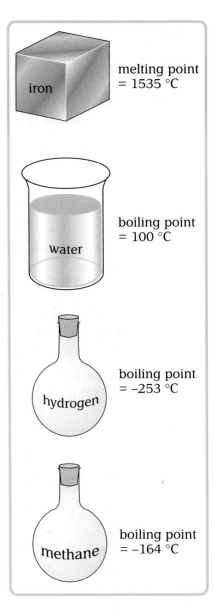

iron   melting point = 1535 °C

water   boiling point = 100 °C

hydrogen   boiling point = –253 °C

methane   boiling point = –164 °C

You should now understand the key words
and key ideas shown below.

- An **element** contains only one type of **atom**.

- A **compound** contains different types of atoms joined together.

- The formula of a substance tells us the number of each type of atom present in the substance.

- The properties of a compound are different from those of the elements which it contains.

- A compound is a pure substance which is made of the same particles.

- A sample of a compound will always have the same elements present in the same fixed proportions.

- Compounds will **react** chemically to make new substances.

- You can tell that a compound has reacted by observing what happens to it.

- A **mixture** is formed when two or more pure substances are added together.

- Air is a mixture of gases that can be separated into pure substances.

- Air consists of **nitrogen**, **oxygen**, **argon** (and other noble gases), **carbon dioxide** and **water vapour**.

- Each of the gases found in air has important uses.

- Air can be **liquefied** and then the individual gases can be separated by **fractional distillation**.

- Sea water and mineral water are other examples of mixtures.

- Elements and compounds melt and boil at a certain temperature.

- Mixtures do not melt or boil at one particular temperature.

- The **melting point** and **boiling point** of a mixture change as the composition of the mixture changes.

Rocks and weathering

In this unit you will learn about rocks and how the materials that rocks are made of are recycled by weathering, erosion and deposition. These natural processes happen over a long period of time.

KEY WORDS
minerals
textures
porous
non-porous
weathering
limestone
chemical weathering
sedimentary rocks
sandstone
igneous rock
granite
erosion
deposition
sediments
abrasion
fossils
millions of years

8G.1 Rocks vary

Scientists who study rocks are called <u>geologists</u>. We sometimes say that something is 'as hard as a rock', but not all rocks are hard. Geologists call <u>all</u> the materials in the photographs rocks.

 1 Sort the rocks into two groups; solid rocks and loose-grained rocks (soft like sand).

Most rocks are made of a mixture of grains of different sizes. The grains can be made of different substances which we call **minerals**.

 2 Write down:

    a <u>one</u> rock with a mixture of small and large grains;

    b <u>one</u> rock with small grains;

    c <u>one</u> rock that is clearly made of a mixture of minerals.

Geologists sort rocks into two groups, according to the way the grains fit together. They say that the two groups have different **textures**. In one group, the grains have small spaces between them, called pores, so we call them **porous** rocks. In the other group, the grains fit closely together with no spaces or pores. So we say that they are **non-porous**.

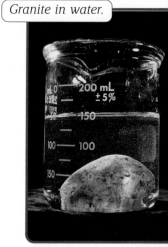

Granite in water.

Look at the photographs.

3   Is granite or sandstone the porous rock? Explain your answers.

4   What do you think is in the pores of porous rocks?

5   In some places we can drill boreholes in rocks to get water or oil. Do we find water and oil in porous rocks or in non-porous rocks? Explain your answer.

Sandstone in water.

6   Gas and oil rise through pore spaces in rocks. Geologists searching for gas and oil look for structures that act as 'traps'. These traps stop the gas and oil moving up further. Find out what these traps are like.

8G.2 Rock and rain

Rocks don't stay the same for ever. Over a long period of time, rain, frost, temperature changes and wind all help to change rocks and break them down. Look at the photograph. The weather caused the change to the old gargoyle. So we call the process **weathering**.

1   a Describe the differences between the old and the new gargoyles.

   b How long did these changes take?

this gargoyle has just been replaced

this gargoyle is 500 years old

Explaining weathering

Rainwater is one of the main causes of weathering. You probably know that rain is slightly acidic. In Unit 7F, you learned that acids react with carbonates and with other substances.

- The gargoyles are made of **limestone**.
- Limestone is made of calcium carbonate.
- Acidic rain reacts with the calcium carbonate.
- One of the products is carbon dioxide. It escapes into the air.
- The other product dissolves, so it is washed away.
- So the limestone weathers.

The reaction between rain and the limestone is a chemical reaction. So we call this kind of weathering **chemical weathering**.

2 Explain where the missing bits of the gargoyle went.

Limestones and sandstones are formed as loose deposits or sediments in the sea. They are called **sedimentary rocks**. Material called cement holds the grains together and makes the rock solid. In some types of **sandstones**, the grains of sand are held together with a cement of calcium carbonate. The pictures show what happens when you soak this kind of sandstone in acid.

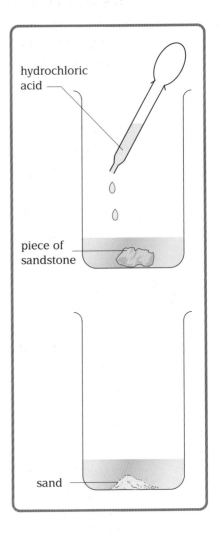

hydrochloric acid

piece of sandstone

sand

3 Explain how chemical weathering turns some sandstones into a pile of sand.

4 The grains in the sandstone in the picture fell apart in about half an hour. Explain why it takes rain many years to break down sandstone.

Weathering very hard rocks

Deep down in the Earth, it is very hot. Sometimes the rocks there get so hot that they melt. We call the melted rocks magma. When magma cools, it becomes solid rock again. We call this new kind of rock an **igneous rock**. **Granite** is an igneous rock.

The crystals in granite fit closely together, so it is a hard, non-porous rock.

5 Look closely at the minerals in granite.
- quartz: semi-transparent (glassy) crystals;
- feldspars: large pink or white crystals;
- mica: small, black crystals.

Draw and label <u>one</u> crystal of each mineral.

Rainwater reacts with feldspars and micas and changes them into new substances. This is chemical weathering. Some of the products are soluble so they dissolve in the water and are washed away.

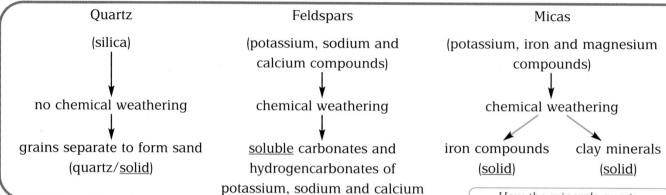

Quartz	Feldspars	Micas
(silica)	(potassium, sodium and calcium compounds)	(potassium, iron and magnesium compounds)
↓	↓	↓
no chemical weathering	chemical weathering	chemical weathering
↓	↓	
grains separate to form sand (quartz/<u>solid</u>)	<u>soluble</u> carbonates and hydrogencarbonates of potassium, sodium and calcium	iron compounds (<u>solid</u>) clay minerals (<u>solid</u>)

How the minerals quartz, feldspars and micas in granite are weathered by rain.

You don't need to learn the names of these chemicals, but you do need to know that rain weathers the three minerals in different ways.

6 Look at the chart for the weathering of granite. Write down:

a <u>two</u> minerals that rain changes by chemical weathering;

b <u>two</u> products of chemical weathering that are washed away.

7 a When granite weathers, which <u>two</u> solids are left behind?

b Which one is in the same form as in the original granite?

8 Look at the photograph of the gargoyles on page 78. If these statues were made of granite, you would be able to feel little hollows where one of the minerals was washed away.

Explain this as fully as you can.

9 Basalt is another hard, igneous rock. Look at the table.

A thin section of basalt

Mineral	Approximate % of mineral in	
	Granite	**Basalt**
quartz	38	3
feldspars	47	57
micas and other iron and magnesium minerals	15	40

Tanya soaked 100 g blocks of granite and basalt in concentrated acid for a month. Which one left the largest mass of solids at the end? Explain your answer.

8G.3 Rocks and temperature changes

What happens when water in rocks freezes?

When water changes to ice it takes up more space. We say that it <u>expands</u>.

The water in this bottle changed to ice.

 1 Look at the picture. What else happened when the water turned to ice?

Most rocks have cracks in them that can fill up with water. When this water freezes, it expands. This means that the cracks widen. The change is very small, so it is hard to tell that it has happened. But when the ice melts, the rock breaks into pieces.

a Look at the cracks in this shale.

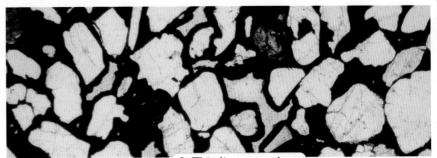

b This limestone has pores and cracks.

 2 Explain how water freezing in cracks in rocks causes weathering.

water

Water inside the crack freezes and expands.

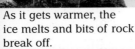

As it gets warmer, the ice melts and bits of rock break off.

 3 It is safer for mountaineers to climb early in the morning than at midday. Explain this as fully as you can.

4 Mountain peaks and the rocks that fall from mountains are not rounded. They have sharp angles. Why do you think this is?

5 Explain how the screes in the Alps formed.

Some screes in the Alps

What happens as rocks heat up and cool down?

Expansion of the rock itself causes weathering. If you have studied *Spectrum Physics* Unit 8I, you will know that:

● when we heat up a substance, the particles in it move faster and take up more space. So the space that the whole substance takes up increases – we say that it expands;

● when a substance cools down, the particles move more slowly and take up less space. The substance contracts.

6 The particles in a solid are close together.
Draw diagrams to show the difference between the particles in an expanded solid and a contracted solid.

In sunny places, rocks get hot during the day and cool down at night. So they expand and contract over and over again.
The large forces resulting from expansion and contraction make the rock crack.

7 Look at the picture. Which part of the rock gets hottest?

At the surface the rock
• heats up first;
• cools down first;
• expands the most.

Just below the surface the rock
• heats up less;
• cools more slowly.

In the middle of the rock, the temperature of the rock hardly changes.

8 **a** Copy the outline of the rock in the picture. Shade the part of the rock that you think will crack.

 b Explain why you chose that part.

 c Draw some cracks in red.

9 The kind of weathering shown in the picture is sometimes called <u>onion skin weathering</u>.
Why do you think this is?
Hint: Think about peeling an onion.

Very hot days and very cold nights caused this weathering.

8G.4 Moving weathered pieces of rock

As a result of weathering, rocks break down into bits that we call <u>rock fragments</u>. Sometimes forces move them away from where they formed. We call this **erosion**.

Gravity makes loose rock fragments fall or roll down slopes. Gravity makes water flow downhill too. Rainwater washes down smaller rock fragments. Then water currents in rivers carry them away.

In the hills, streams flow quickly. Streams carry smaller rock fragments away and leave the large fragments behind.

1 Weathering and erosion are different processes. Explain the effect of the two processes on a rock.

2 One force that causes erosion is gravity. Explain <u>two</u> ways that gravity helps to move rock fragments.

When rock fragments settle, we call this process **deposition**. We call the deposits **sediments**. The pictures show the sediments deposited at different stages of a river's journey.

3 Look at the pictures. Describe the sediments in each picture.

4 Write down <u>two</u> ways that the fragments upstream are different from the fragments lower down.

Further downstream, we see beaches made of pebbles.

Sediments are not all the same size

The slope of a river bed changes along its course. Look at the diagram.

HILLS
→ gentler slope
→ current flows more slowly
→ current has less energy to carry grains
→ smaller grains are carried further

SEA

5 Why does the water flow more quickly in the hills?

On flatter land, the river flows more slowly so it deposits sand.

6 **a** In what way does the speed of the current affect the size of the fragments that it can move?

b Explain why the speed of the current has this effect.

7 In the hills, the fragments of rock that fall into streams are a mixture of different sizes. But the ones on the bed of the stream are all large. Where do the smaller fragments go?

8 The river deposits sand in one place and mud in another. It seems to sort the sediment grains into similar sizes. Describe how it does this.

The river deposits fine sand and mud as it gets nearer to the sea.

Why the shapes of rock fragments change

When weathered rock fragments form, they are angular. As the water moves them along, the fragments knock against each other. Corners get knocked off and they become more rounded. The water lifts up smaller grains and dashes them against other fragments causing wear. We call this wear **abrasion**. It is a bit like sand blasting. In a river, the sand blasting effect makes the rock fragments smoother and more rounded.

 9 What is abrasion?

 10 What is the connection between the shape of rock fragments and the distance they travel?

 11 Find out how we use abrasion <u>either</u> to clean old buildings <u>or</u> to polish decorative stones.

8G.5 Why sediments form layers

In the last topic, you learned that rivers move sediments and that the sediments settle when the water doesn't have enough energy to carry them. This means that sometimes a river carries larger particles than at other times.

 1 These pictures show the same river. Write down the differences between the two pictures. Include differences in speed of flow, and size and number of particles carried.

a The river carries only very small particles of sediment when it is flowing slowly.

b The river is in flood. When it flows quickly it carries a lot of sediment.

2 Look at the beaker of water and sand. Why does the sand settle when you stop stirring?

3 Look at what happens when the particles are a mixture of sizes. Describe what you see.

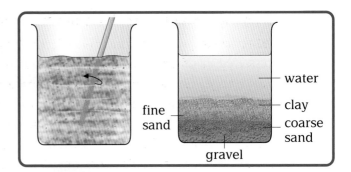

fine sand

water
clay
coarse sand
gravel

4 Now look at the rocks in the cliff. Are the layers more, or less, clear than in the jar?

The distinct layers show that different sediments settle at different times.

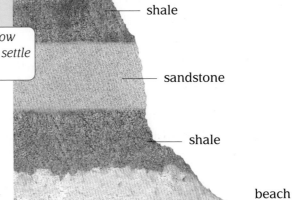

shale

sandstone

shale

beach

How the layers in the cliff formed

The rocks in the cliff formed from sediments deposited in the sea. They are sedimentary rocks. When a river reaches the sea, the water slows down and it deposits its load of sediments.

Look at the picture. A layer of mud settled first. It formed the shale, so the shale is the oldest rock. It took many years to form. The top of this layer marks a time when deposition of sediment stopped. Later, deposits of sand formed the sandstone.

5 In the cliff, which is the youngest layer of rock and what is it made from? Explain your answers.

6 What do the layers of sand and mud tell you about the changes in speed of the river that brought them into the sea?

7 **a** Which of the layers of sediment probably took the longest to form? Explain your answer.

   b Why can't you be sure that you are right?

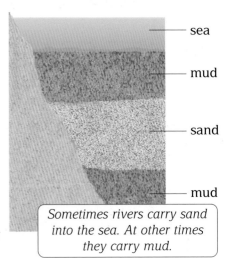

sea

mud

sand

mud

Sometimes rivers carry sand into the sea. At other times they carry mud.

The rocks in the cliff are harder than new sediments in the sea. But the new sediments will harden in time. The weight of newer layers presses down on the older ones and squeezes water out. Dissolved solids from the water form crystals that cement the sediments together. The dissolved solids in rivers, lakes and seas come from weathered rock.

8 Explain how the rock fragments that make up a sediment become cemented together.

Some rocks form mainly from dissolved solids

How dissolved solids become concentrated in seas and lakes.

rain

chemical weathering of rocks

dissolved salts in rivers

water evaporate leaving salts behind

sea

9 Look at the diagram.

 a What kind of weathering produces dissolved solids?

 b How do these substances reach the sea?

 c Why is the concentration of dissolved solids much higher in the sea than in rivers?

Water evaporates from this soda lake faster than it flows in. As water evaporates, crystals of salts are deposited.

10 What makes the water evaporate from seas and lakes?

11 Salt deposits form in some seas and lakes but not in others.

 Explain this as fully as you can.

Living things form rocks too

Many animals take dissolved solids out of the water to make their shell or skeleton. When the animals die, these hard parts don't decay; they form sediments too.

Corals and molluscs are two groups of animals that make their hard parts from calcium carbonate.

12 Write down <u>two</u> animals that concentrate dissolved solids.

13 Write down the name of the chemical that forms the hard parts of these animals.

14 a What happens to the soft parts of animals when they die?

 b What happens to the hard parts when the animals die?

 c What kind of sedimentary rock do they form?

You can still see the shells and other hard parts of animals in these limestones. We call them **fossils**.

Stories in rocks

When we know what to look for, rocks can tell us something of the history of a place over **millions of years**. But it wasn't until the 18th and 19th centuries that people started to realise this.

James Hutton, a British geologist who lived from 1726 to 1797, had a theory that rocks formed in the past in the same ways that they form today. We can use this idea to work out whether a rock formed in the sea, in a lake or in a desert. For example, corals live only where the sea is clear, warm and fairly shallow. So rocks that contain corals must have formed in the same conditions.

In a river delta mud is carried to the sea and settles in layers. This photograph was taken from a Space Shuttle.

 15 If you find a fossil coral in a rock, what does this tell you about the environment at the time the rock formed?

 16 How do we know that the rock in the photograph formed in a delta?

Fossils also help to tell the story

Fossil collecting was popular in the nineteenth century. Mary Anning was one of the best-known fossil hunters. She, and her brother Joseph, found the first complete fossil of an ichthyosaur.

William Smith used fossils to help him to make the first geological map of England and Wales. His idea was that rocks with the same fossils in them are the same age. So he used fossils to match rocks in different parts of the country to help him to make his maps.

This rock formed in a river delta. The stripes in the rock are called <u>current bedding</u>.

 17 Another of William Smith's ideas was, 'Of any two strata [layers of rock], that which was originally below is the older.' What did he mean?

Telling the story

Look at the drawing. The rocks in the cliff took millions of years to form.

 18 Draw a diagram to show the layers in the cliff face. Write on the diagram the names of the rocks. Then label:

a the oldest layer;

b a layer formed in a clear sea;

c a layer formed when a river brought lots of sand into the sea;

d a layer formed when the sea dried up;

e a layer formed in a river delta.

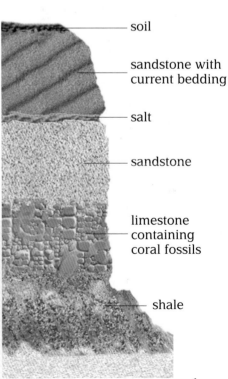

soil

sandstone with current bedding

salt

sandstone

limestone containing coral fossils

shale

You should now understand the key words and key ideas shown below.

ROCKS are made of a mixture of **mineral** grains.

We call the way grains fit together the **texture**.

- In a **non-porous** rock, grains fit closely together.

- In a **porous** rock, they have spaces between them.

Rocks such as **sandstone** and **limestone** form when sediments settle. They are **sedimentary** rocks.
Rocks such as **granite** form when magma solidifies.
They are **igneous** rocks.

Weathering breaks down rocks.

Water causes **chemical weathering** of some minerals.

Mechanical weathering is caused by:

- temperature changes,

- water expanding as it freezes.

We call the transport of rock fragments **erosion**.

The faster a river flows, the larger the fragments that it can carry.

The further rock fragments travel, the smaller and smoother they become. Wearing of rocks by sand is called **abrasion**.

When rock fragments settle and form layers, we call it deposition.

Sediments are **deposited** as rivers slow down.

When a river reaches the sea, it slows down so much that even the smallest rock fragments are deposited.

The boundary between two layers of rock represents a time when deposition stopped.

The remains of dead organisms (**fossils**) sometimes form deposits.

Evaporation of water causes deposition of dissolved solids.

Remember:

- When we study the Earth we can look at processes that are happening now, and work out what happened in the past.

- These processes are very slow. They take place over **millions of years**.

The rock cycle

In this unit you will be finding out more about different types of rocks, how rocks form and how the materials in rocks are used over and over again, both on the Earth's surface and deep under the ground.

KEY WORDS

sediment
sedimentary rocks
fossils
metamorphic
aligned
magma
igneous
basalt
granite
obsidian
pumice
lava
erupts
volcanoes
volcanic ash
gabbro

8H.1 How sedimentary rocks form

In Unit 8G, you learned how James Hutton (1726–97) taught us that looking at what is happening to rocks now helps us to understand what happened to rocks in the past.

You looked at how:

- the weather breaks down rocks;

- rivers transport the rock fragments to the sea;

- layers of **sediment** are laid down on top of one another on the sea bed.

All these things are happening now. They have happened for over 4000 million years.

Rocks made from sediments are called **sedimentary rocks**.

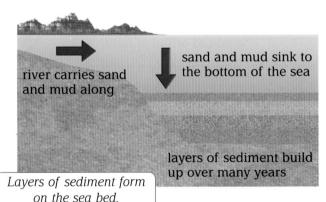

river carries sand and mud along

sand and mud sink to the bottom of the sea

layers of sediment build up over many years

Layers of sediment form on the sea bed.

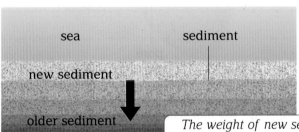

sea

sediment

new sediment

older sediment

The weight of new sediments presses down on the older sediments. This pressure squeezes water out and compresses the sediments. Chemical changes cement the fragments together, forming solid rock.

1 What are sedimentary rocks?

2 Write a paragraph about how sediments change into sedimentary rocks.

8H.3 Rocks are sometimes changed

Sometimes new rocks form when existing rocks are changed without being melted. We call the new rocks **metamorphic** rocks.

- If you see a word with 'meta' in, it means change.

- 'Morph' in a word means form.

- So a 'metamorphic' rock is a rock with a changed form.

We call the process **metamorphism**.

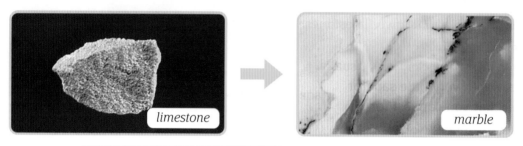

You can see rounded grains and pores in limestone. Marble is harder, with a granular, sugary texture and no pore spaces.

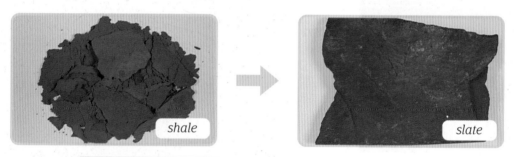

Shale is soft and crumbly, but slate is hard. The minerals in slate are lined up in the same direction.

Sandstone is made up of grains of sand. Quartzite is harder with a sugary texture.

1   What is a metamorphic rock?

2   Write down the names of <u>three</u> metamorphic rocks.

3 Are metamorphic rocks porous or non-porous?
Explain your answer.

4 Look at the photographs on page 92. Write down
<u>three</u> types of changes that happen as a result of
metamorphism.

What causes the changes?

Heat or pressure, or a mixture of the two, can change rocks.

- <u>Pressure</u> lines up thin, flat, plate-like minerals in the same
direction. We say that they have become **aligned**.

- <u>High temperatures</u> cause reactions that chemically change
some of the minerals in the rocks.

All these changes happen in the solid state. The rocks do not melt.

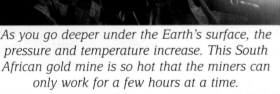

*As you go deeper under the Earth's surface, the
pressure and temperature increase. This South
African gold mine is so hot that the miners can
only work for a few hours at a time.*

*This molten lava heats up the
surrounding rocks.*

5 Write down <u>two</u> ways that rocks get hot enough to
change them.

6 Write down <u>two</u> ways that pressure is put on rocks in
the Earth.

7 What do you think happened to change the shale
into slate?

*Movements of the Earth's
crust cause heating and
squashing of rocks.*

8H.4 Rocks formed from molten magma

When you heat ice, it melts to form water. When you cool the water to 0 °C, it solidifies again. We call 0 °C the melting point of ice. It is also the freezing point of water.

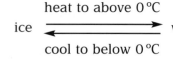

heat to above 0 °C

ice ⇌ water

cool to below 0 °C

Deep in the Earth, the rocks sometimes get so hot that they reach their melting point. We call molten rock **magma**. For example, the melting point of granite is about 1000 °C. When magma cools to below 1000 °C, it solidifies, but it is still very hot. Other rocks melt at different temperatures.

1   Draw a diagram, like the one for ice, to show what happens to granite above and below 1000 °C.

a sandstone

Magma is a mixture of minerals. When magma solidifies, it usually forms crystals. You can see crystals of different minerals in most rocks formed from magma. We call rocks formed from magma **igneous** rocks.

2   What is:

   a magma;

   b igneous rock?

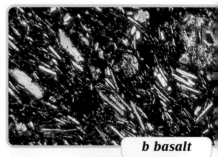

b basalt

3   Look at the photographs of the three rocks.
   Which <u>two</u> are igneous rocks? Explain your answer.

4   Write down <u>one</u> difference between the two igneous rocks.

c granite

Crystal size in igneous rocks

In Unit 7H, you made crystals of salt by evaporating water from a solution.

5   **a** What does 'evaporating' mean?

   b What affects the size of the crystals formed when water evaporates from a solution?

   c How do you make large crystals?

these crystals formed quickly   these crystals formed slowly

The size of the crystals depends on how quickly you evaporate the water from the solution.

As magma solidifies, it is the rate of cooling that affects crystal size. When magma cools slowly, the crystals have a long time to form. So the crystals are larger than when magma cools quickly. Sometimes magma cools so quickly that there is no time at all for crystals to form.

6 Look back at the photographs of granite and basalt. Did granite or basalt form from magma that cooled quickly? Explain your answer.

Some magmas cool more quickly than others

Molten magma rises up through the Earth's crust.

Obsidian is glassy, not crystalline, so it is sometimes called volcanic glass.

- Some magmas cool and solidify while they are still deep underground. They are surrounded by hot rock, so they cool slowly.

- Some magmas solidify in cracks in rocks or between layers of other rocks nearer to the Earth's surface. They cool more quickly.

- Others magmas are still molten when they come out onto the surface. They cool very quickly.

7 Look at the pictures of obsidian and pumice. Describe how and where each of them probably formed.

8 Look back at the photographs of granite and basalt. Which one formed deep underground? Explain your answer.

You can see gas bubbles trapped in pumice, but no crystals.

We call magma that reaches the surface of the Earth **lava**. When lava comes out onto the surface of the Earth we say that it **erupts**. Some lavas are very runny so they form lava flows that spread out in layers over large areas.

Lava flows out of a volcano called Kilauea, in Hawaii

Less runny lavas form **volcanoes**. Sometimes magma solidifies inside the volcano. Gases are trapped underneath the solid magma. The pressure builds up until the gases, solids and more molten lava burst out of the top like the froth from a shaken fizzy drink. These materials form a cloud which settles as a **volcanic ash** cone. Eruptions can happen on land, into the sea or even under the sea.

Mount St. Helens is an ash cone. Ash is blown out of this volcano in a cloud.

9 Describe the shape of a volcano.

10 Write down <u>two</u> substances that volcanoes are made from.

11 Describe how the volcano in the drawing was formed.

12 Surtsey first appeared as a cloud of steam in the sea. Explain this as fully as you can.

13 Find out when Surtsey appeared out of the sea. Then use an atlas to find out where it is.

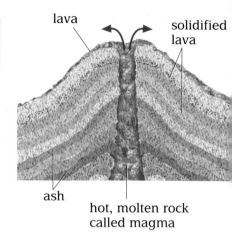

lava
solidified lava
ash
hot, molten rock called magma

Some volcanic cones form from ash and lava.

The minerals in magmas vary too

Mineral	Percentage composition	
	Gabbro	Granite
silica	49.9	70.8
aluminium oxide	16.0	14.6
iron and magnesium minerals	18.2	4.3
other minerals	15.9	10.3

Surtsey erupted under the sea and formed a new island.

Gabbro

Granite

14 Write down <u>one</u> piece of evidence that both rocks:

a are igneous rocks;

b formed deep below the Earth's surface.

8H.5 Recycling rocks

In this unit you have learned that you can classify rocks as sedimentary, igneous and metamorphic.

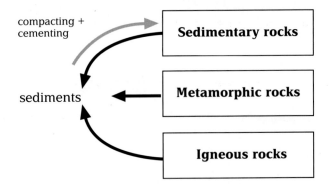

Sediments are deposits of rock fragments. They form as a result of weathering, erosion and deposition. Sedimentary rocks form by compacting and cementing of the sediments.

1   Which colour of arrow on the diagram shows

    a weathering, erosion and deposition;

    b compacting and cementing?

Magma is molten rock. Igneous rocks form when magma cools and solidifies.

Rocks changed by heat and pressure are called metamorphic rocks.

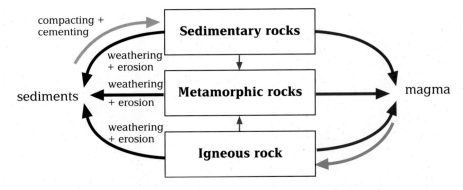

2   What colour are the arrows that show:

    a melting;

    b cooling and solidifying;

    c heat and pressure?

So, the minerals in rocks are used over and over again for millions of years. In other words, they are recycled.

3   What name do we give to the recycling of rocks?

You should now understand the key words and key ideas shown below.

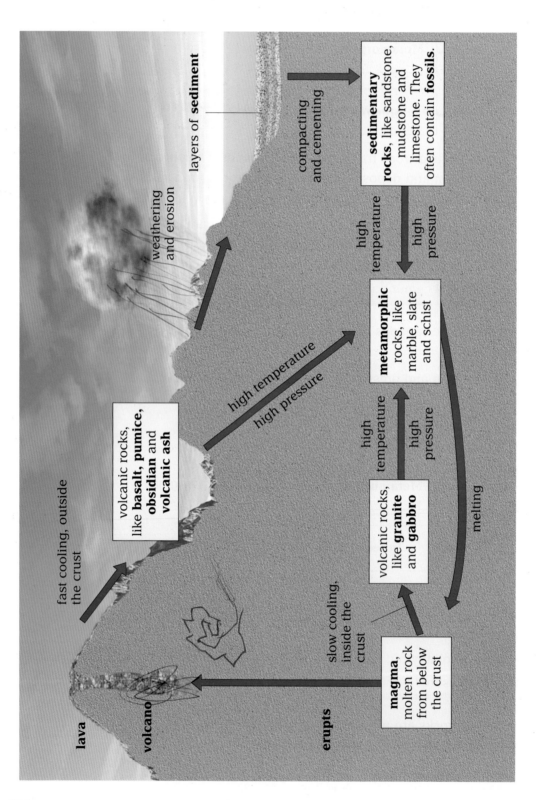

sedimentary rocks, like sandstone, mudstone and limestone. They often contain **fossils**.

layers of **sediment**

compacting and cementing

weathering and erosion

high temperature

high pressure

metamorphic rocks, like marble, slate and schist

high temperature

high pressure

volcanic rocks, like **basalt, pumice, obsidian** and **volcanic ash**

high temperature

high pressure

volcanic rocks, like **granite** and **gabbro**

melting

fast cooling, outside the crust

slow cooling, inside the crust

lava

volcano

erupts

magma, molten rock from below the crust

Reactions of metals and metal compounds

In this unit we shall be learning about the properties of metals and their compounds. We shall also explore how metals and metal compounds react with acids.

9E.1 Why are metals useful?

Although **metals** vary, they all have some things in common. These things are called the **properties** of metals.

have <u>high melting points</u> so are solid at room temperature

are <u>shiny</u> when polished

are <u>dense</u>

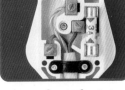
are <u>good conductors of electricity</u>

Properties of metals

can be <u>hammered</u> and <u>bent</u> into shape; are usually <u>tough</u> and <u>strong</u>

are <u>good conductors of heat</u>

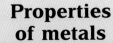
have <u>alkaline oxides</u>

form mixtures of metals called <u>alloys</u>

only three metals are <u>magnetic</u>, iron, nickel and cobalt

The properties of metals

1   Write down <u>six</u> properties that <u>all</u> metals have in common.

2   What property makes iron, cobalt and nickel special?

Although metals have properties in common, there is variation between them. That is why we use different metals for different jobs.

3 Explain why we use copper for pipes and wiring in our homes.

4 Explain how particular properties of aluminium determine its uses.

5 Explain why gold jewellery stays shiny for a long time.

6 Explain why iron is used to make cooking pans.

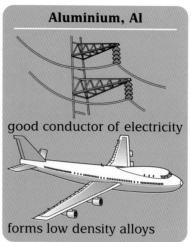

Aluminium, Al

good conductor of electricity

forms low density alloys

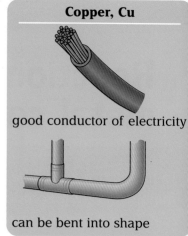

Copper, Cu

good conductor of electricity

can be bent into shape

Gold, Au

unreactive, so stays shiny for a long time

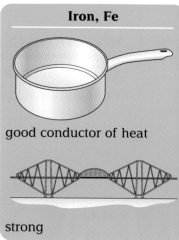

Iron, Fe

good conductor of heat

strong

Some uses of metals

Properties of non-metals

You could say that **non-metals** have the opposite properties to metals.

Properties of metals	Properties of non-metals
have high melting points	have low melting and boiling points
are shiny	are dull
can be hammered and bent into shape	are usually brittle when solid
are good conductors of heat	are poor conductors of heat (are insulators)
are good conductors of electricity	are poor conductors of electricity (are insulators)
form alloys	do not form alloys
iron, nickel and cobalt are magnetic	no non-metals are magnetic

7 What name is given to a substance that does not let electricity pass through it?

8 What name is given to a substance that does not let heat pass through it?

Metal or non-metal?

Once you have found out its properties, it is usually easy to work out if an element is a metal or a non-metal. However, you need to be careful! Some metals and non-metals have unexpected properties:

- Mercury is a metal that is a liquid at room temperature.

- Graphite (a form of carbon) is a non-metal that is a good conductor of electricity.

- Diamond (another form of carbon) is a non-metal that is the hardest known natural substance.

When you are trying to decide if an element is a metal or a non-metal, you need to look at more than one property.

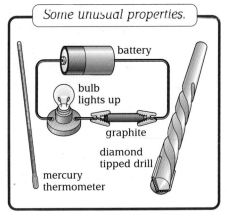

Some unusual properties.

Property	Element X
appearance	shiny, dark-grey solid
melting point	1410 °C
electrical conductivity	medium
thermal (heat) conductivity	low

 9 Name a non-metal that conducts electricity.

 10 What property of mercury enables it to be used in thermometers?

 11 Look at the table. Is element X a metal or a non-metal? Explain your answer.

Physical and chemical properties

The properties that we have looked at so far describe what an element is like. These are its **physical properties**. An element's **chemical properties** describe how it reacts. The pictures shown an example.

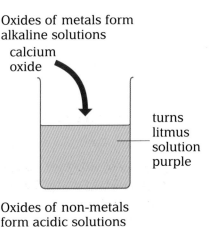

Oxides of metals form alkaline solutions

calcium oxide

turns litmus solution purple

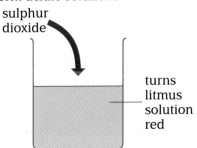

Oxides of non-metals form acidic solutions

sulphur dioxide

turns litmus solution red

 12 Does calcium oxide form acidic or alkaline solutions?

 13 Some sulphur dioxide is dissolved in water to form a solution. What is the pH of this solution?

9E.2 Reacting metals with acids

We have seen that metals vary. Particular combinations of properties make different metals suitable for different jobs. It would be no use making a saucepan out of a metal that then explodes when it is heated up or reacts when you put water in it!

Metals and acids

Look at the pictures and the table.

Name of acid	Formula
hydrochloric acid	HCl
sulphuric acid	H_2SO_4

 1 What is the evidence in the pictures for chemical reactions?

 2 Describe the test for hydrogen. (Remember from Unit 7F.)

Hydrogen is not the only product of reactions between metals and acids. Salts are always produced. Look at the picture.

What we need to do now is name the salt. We can do this by writing word and symbol equations for what we know about the reaction:

zinc + sulphuric acid → hydrogen + ...

$$Zn + H_2SO_4 \rightarrow H_2 + ...$$

There is no Zn or SO_4 on the right-hand side of the equation. The Zn and the SO_4 join together to make the salt, $ZnSO_4$, called zinc sulphate.

word equation:

zinc + sulphuric acid → zinc sulphate + hydrogen

symbol equation:

$$Zn + H_2SO_4 \rightarrow ZnSO_4 + H_2$$

 3 What is the name of the salt produced when zinc reacts with sulphuric acid?

 4 Name the elements found in sulphuric acid.

zinc reacting with...

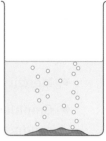

hydrochloric acid

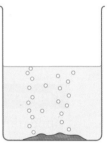

sulphuric acid

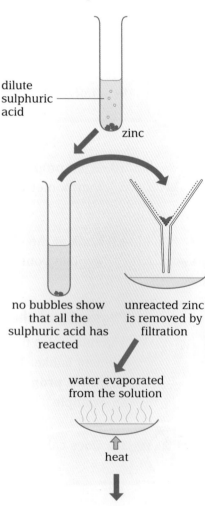

dilute sulphuric acid

zinc

no bubbles show that all the sulphuric acid has reacted

unreacted zinc is removed by filtration

water evaporated from the solution

heat

crystals of salt are left

Getting the salt

Metals and acids – word equations

We know that most metals react with acids in a similar way. The general word equation is:

metal + acid → salt + hydrogen

All we have to work out is the name of the salt formed in the reaction. This is done by taking the name of metal and adding the name of the acid to it.

Name of acid	Name of salt produced
sulphuric acid	sulphate
hydrochloric acid	chloride
nitric acid	nitrate

We can now work out the name of the salt using the names of the metal and the acid. For example:

zinc + sulphuric acid → zinc sulphate + hydrogen

calcium + hydrochloric acid → calcium chloride + hydrogen

magnesium + nitric acid → magnesium nitrate + hydrogen

5 Name the salt formed when:

   a potassium reacts with sulphuric acid;

   b magnesium reacts with hydrochloric acid.

6 What acid would you use to make:

   a iron chloride and hydrogen from iron;

   b calcium nitrate and hydrogen from calcium?

7 Describe how you would prove that a salt forms when magnesium reacts with dilute hydrochloric acid.

9E.3 Reacting metal carbonates with acids

In chemistry we find there are several 'groups' of atoms which are often found together in chemical compounds. Nitrates, sulphates and carbonates are examples. We are going to explore how **metal carbonates** react with acids. Metal carbonates are chemical compounds made from a metal and the carbonate group, CO_3.

1 Name the elements found in calcium carbonate.

At the end of the reaction in the pictures a blue solution is formed. This is a salt called copper sulphate.

2 Look at the pictures. Write down <u>three</u> signs that a chemical reaction is happening.

3 The gas produced turns limewater milky white. Name the gas.

4 The symbol equation for this reaction is:
$$CuCO_3 + H_2SO_4 \longrightarrow CuSO_4 + H_2O + CO_2$$
Write the word equation.

All metal carbonates react with acids in a similar way. The chemical reaction between a metal carbonate and an acid always produces a salt, water and carbon dioxide. We can write a general word equation:

metal carbonate + acid → salt + water + carbon dioxide

5 Which gas is always produced when a metal carbonate reacts with an acid?

6 Name the salt formed when:

a iron carbonate reacts with sulphuric acid;

b magnesium carbonate reacts with nitric acid.

7 What reactants would you use to make:

a iron chloride, water and carbon dioxide;

b magnesium sulphate, water and carbon dioxide?

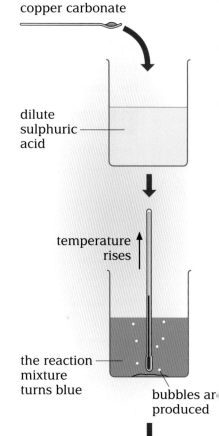

Copper carbonate and dilute sulphuric acid react to form copper sulphate.

copper carbonate

dilute sulphuric acid

temperature rises

the reaction mixture turns blue

bubbles are produced

copper sulphate solution

once the reaction stops bubbling, the unreacted copper carbonate is removed by filtration

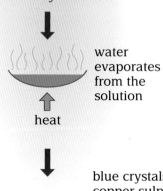

water evaporates from the solution

heat

blue crystals of copper sulphate are left

9E.4 Reacting metal oxides with acids

Many metal **ores** are oxides.

1 Name the element which is found in all metal oxides.

Name of metal oxide	Formula
copper oxide	CuO
sodium oxide	Na$_2$O
zinc oxide	ZnO

The diagrams show the reaction between copper oxide and dilute sulphuric acid.

2 Describe how you can see that the copper oxide has reacted with the dilute sulphuric acid.

3 What method of separation is used to remove unreacted copper oxide from the solution?

The word equation for the reaction shown is:

copper oxide + sulphuric acid → copper sulphate + water

The symbol equation is:

$$CuO \quad + \quad H_2SO_4 \quad \rightarrow \quad CuSO_4 \quad + \quad H_2O$$

4 Why were there no bubbles in this reaction?

All **metal oxides** react with acids in a similar way. The chemical reaction between a metal oxide and an acid always produces a salt and water, so we can write a general word equation:

metal oxide + acid → salt + water

We can now predict what is made in the chemical reaction between any metal oxide and any acid.

5 Name the products of a reaction between a metal oxide and an acid.

6 Name the salt formed when:

   a zinc oxide reacts with sulphuric acid;

   b iron oxide reacts with hydrochloric acid.

7 What reactants would you use to make:

   a copper chloride and water;

   b magnesium sulphate and water?

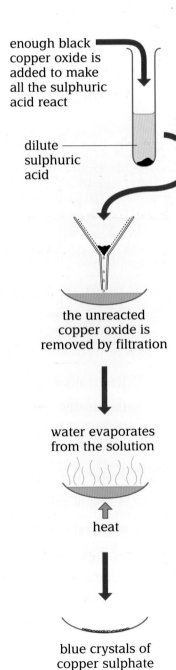

enough black copper oxide is added to make all the sulphuric acid react

dilute sulphuric acid

the unreacted copper oxide is removed by filtration

water evaporates from the solution

heat

blue crystals of copper sulphate are left

9E.5 More about salts

The first part of the name of a salt comes from a metal and the second part comes from an acid.

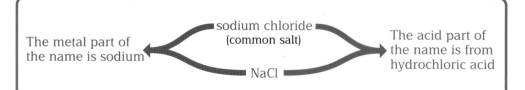

The metal part of the name is sodium

sodium chloride (common salt)

NaCl

The acid part of the name is from hydrochloric acid

Name of salt	Formula
copper sulphate	$CuSO_4$
sodium chloride	NaCl
zinc nitrate	$Zn(NO_3)_2$

Salts have many different uses.

Gunpowder contains potassium nitrate

Copper sulphate, used as a fungicide in agriculture

Epsom salts are magnesium sulphate

Photographic film contains silver nitrate

1 What is the chemical name for 'common salt'?

2 What is <u>one</u> use of potassium nitrate?

Neutralisation reactions

In this unit we have seen three different reactions which produce salts:

● metal + acid

● metal carbonate + acid

● metal oxide + acid

In Unit 7E we used neutralisation reactions to make salts too.

Calamine lotion neutralises the acid in bee stings.

Indigestion tablets neutralise excess stomach acid.

Calcium carbonate neutralises acidic rainwater and soil.

3 Describe <u>one</u> everyday use of a neutralisation reaction.

4 Why is the treatment for bee stings alkaline?

We can make common salt in a neutralisation reaction.
This is the symbol equation:

$$HCl + NaOH \rightarrow NaCl + H_2O$$

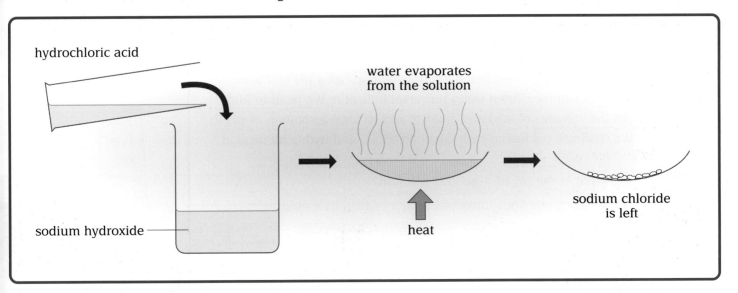

hydrochloric acid

water evaporates
from the solution

sodium chloride
is left

sodium hydroxide

heat

5   Name the type of reaction that happens between dilute
    hydrochloric acid and sodium hydroxide solution.

6   a Write a word equation for the reaction between
      hydrochloric acid and sodium hydroxide.

    b Why don't we see bubbles in this reaction?

7   Name the salt formed when:

    a magnesium hydroxide reacts with sulphuric acid;

    b potassium hydroxide reacts with nitric acid.

8   What reactants would you use to make:

    a calcium chloride and water;

    b sodium sulphate and water?

When we use alkalis in chemical reactions we must make sure we
check their bottles for hazard warning signs. Just like acids, some
alkalis can be dangerous to use. Solutions of alkalis such as
calcium hydroxide are irritants and can cause your skin to
redden, blister and itch. Alkalis such as sodium hydroxide are
corrosive and will attack your skin and start eating it away.

Warning signs.

Neutralisation – an ending

When neutralisation reactions are used in industry it is important that the correct amounts of acid and alkali are used. A product that is acidic or alkaline, when it should be neutral, is not much use. We are going to explore how we find out how much alkali is needed to neutralise an acid.

In Unit 7E you learned that a neutral solution has a pH of 7 and that you can measure it using universal indicator. We need to find out the volumes of acid and alkali to mix to form a solution of pH 7. We shall use potassium hydroxide, an alkali, and hydrochloric acid.

9 What is the pH of a neutral solution?

10 What colour does universal indicator turn in a neutral solution?

Producing a neutral solution

A simple way of producing a neutral solution is to add the potassium hydroxide solution to the dilute hydrochloric acid until the universal indicator turns green. Adding it slowly enough is tricky. One way is to add the potassium hydroxide solution using a dropping pipette.

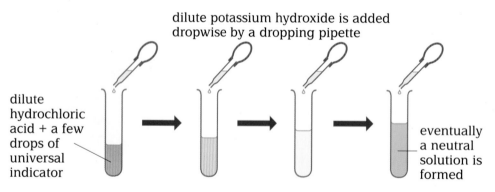

dilute potassium hydroxide is added dropwise by a dropping pipette

dilute hydrochloric acid + a few drops of universal indicator

eventually a neutral solution is formed

However, using a dropping pipette makes it very difficult to measure the exact volume of potassium hydroxide required for the neutralisation. Chemists use a piece of equipment called a burette. It allows them to add the potassium hydroxide solution slowly in precise amounts and to measure the volume accurately.

11 What piece of apparatus do chemists use to measure the exact volume of alkali added to an acid to produce a neutral solution?

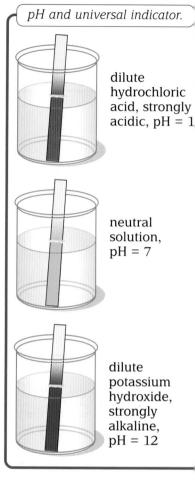

pH and universal indicator.

dilute hydrochloric acid, strongly acidic, pH = 1

neutral solution, pH = 7

dilute potassium hydroxide, strongly alkaline, pH = 12

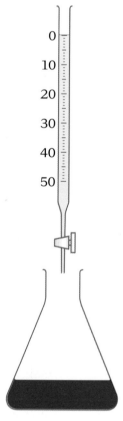

12 Why must the potassium hydroxide solution be added slowly?

13 What happens to the colour of the universal indicator when too much potassium hydroxide solution is added to the dilute hydrochloric acid?

Finding the exact volume

An alternative way is to add the potassium hydroxide solution to the dilute hydrochloric acid $1\,cm^3$ at a time. After each addition of potassium hydroxide solution the mixture is swirled and its pH written down. The pH can be found using universal indicator and a pH card. Alternatively a digital device called a pH probe can be used to get a really accurate measure of the pH. The results of such an experiment are given in the table.

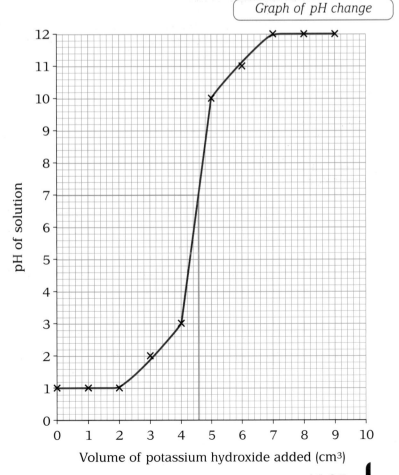

Using a pH probe

Volume of potassium hydroxide added (cm^3)	0	1	2	3	4	5	6	7	8	9
pH of solution	1	1	1	2	3	10	11	12	12	12

The results of this experiment can be plotted as a graph. The graph clearly shows how the pH changes during the neutralisation reaction. A neutral solution is produced when the pH reaches exactly 7. We can use the graph to find out how much potassium hydroxide must be added to the dilute hydrochloric acid to get a solution of exactly pH 7.

Graph of pH change

14 Write down <u>two</u> ways of measuring the pH of a mixture of potassium hydroxide solution and dilute hydrochloric acid.

15 Use the graph to find the exact volume of potassium hydroxide solution needed to neutralise the hydrochloric acid.

pH of solution

Volume of potassium hydroxide added (cm^3)

You should now understand the key words and key ideas shown below.

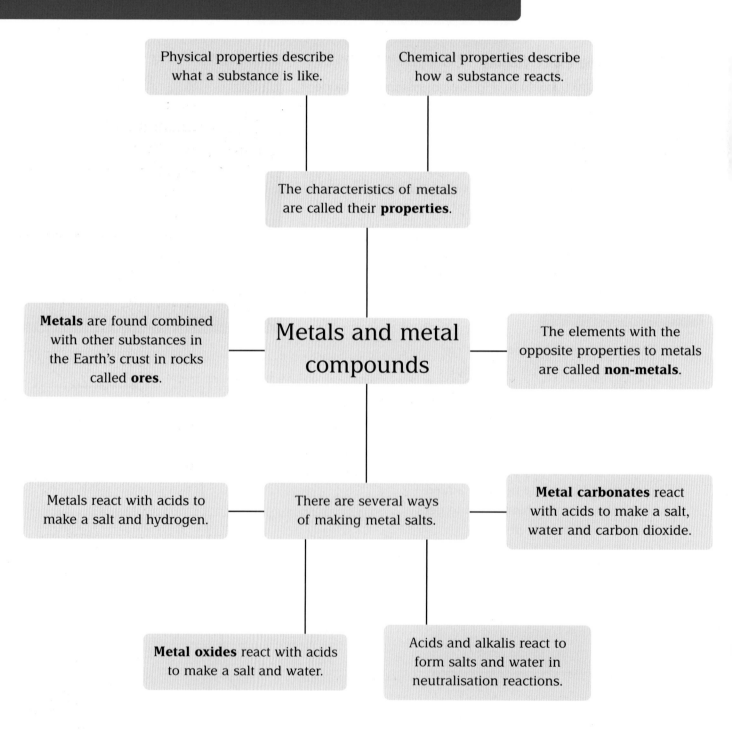

Physical properties describe what a substance is like.

Chemical properties describe how a substance reacts.

The characteristics of metals are called their **properties**.

Metals are found combined with other substances in the Earth's crust in rocks called **ores**.

Metals and metal compounds

The elements with the opposite properties to metals are called **non-metals**.

Metals react with acids to make a salt and hydrogen.

There are several ways of making metal salts.

Metal carbonates react with acids to make a salt, water and carbon dioxide.

Metal oxides react with acids to make a salt and water.

Acids and alkalis react to form salts and water in neutralisation reactions.

Patterns of reactivity

In this unit we shall investigate some reactions of metals and compare their reactivity so that we can put them into a reactivity series. Then we shall use the reactivity series to make predictions about how some metals may react.

KEY WORDS
tarnish
alkali metal
reactivity
reactivity series
predict
salt
displacement reactions
displace
ore
haematite
electrolysis

9F.1 What happens to metals?

Some metals are more reactive than others. When they react with water or other substances in the environment, they change their appearance. We use the metal gold for jewellery because it doesn't change, even over a long period of time. Most other metals don't remain shiny for very long.

When metals change their appearance from a shiny to a dull colour we say they are tarnished. **Tarnish** is a discoloration caused by the reaction between the metal and oxygen. It is an oxidation reaction – a chemical reaction between the metal and its environment. Washing and polishing can remove tarnish, but if you leave any detergent or polish on the surface of the metal, it attracts moisture, leading to a far worse problem – corrosion. Tarnish is not damaging – it is not dirt, and it does not penetrate the surface of metal.

1 Name <u>one</u> metal which does not tarnish easily.

2 What do you think are the properties of copper that make it particularly useful for making pipes?

3 Joy wants to make some jewellery out of iron, but Dan thinks that it would not sell very well. Suggest why iron jewellery is not likely to sell.

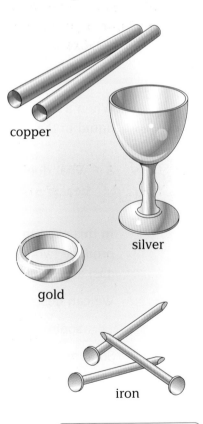

copper

silver

gold

iron

Four different metals.

Metals such as lithium, sodium and potassium tarnish very quickly. A newly cut surface is very shiny, but if you leave the surface exposed it quickly changes to become a dull grey colour.

4 How can you prove that sodium is really a metal?

5 How does the oil protect the metal from tarnishing?

Storing metals such as sodium in oil protects them from tarnishing.

9F.2 Metals and water

Sodium is very reactive with water. When we add a small piece to water it fizzes around the surface producing bubbles of a gas. In a similar reaction with potassium instead of sodium, the reaction produces enough heat for the gas to catch fire.

1 **a** What is the chemical formula of water?

  b What is the chemical symbol for sodium?

The gas produced in this reaction could be oxygen or hydrogen, because both these elements are present in the compound water.

2 Joy thinks that the gas produced is hydrogen and not oxygen. What evidence is there from the experiment to support her idea?

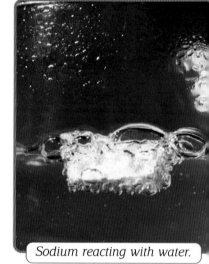

Sodium reacting with water.

When a few drops of universal indicator were added to the liquid in the trough, the indicator turned purple.

3 What does the indicator tell you about the liquid in the beaker at the end of the experiment?

In this experiment the sodium has reacted with the water to produce two new substances. They are hydrogen (the flammable gas) and sodium hydroxide (the alkaline solution).

We can describe this reaction using a word equation:

sodium + water → sodium hydroxide + hydrogen

Sodium, potassium and lithium all produce an alkaline solution. So we call them the **alkali metals**.

4 Work out the word equations for the reaction of:

  a potassium with water;

  b lithium with water.

We know that other metals are not as reactive with water as sodium is. In fact, some metals do not react with water, even after a long time. So these metals are useful for making objects to hold or carry water. Gold, silver and copper are examples.

 5 Give <u>four</u> examples of uses of metals, where the metal needs to be unreactive to water.

Between these extremes of reactivity there are a number of metals that are moderately reactive with water.

 6 Look at the pictures. Which do you think is the more reactive metal, calcium or magnesium?

Some metals, such as iron, zinc and aluminium, don't seem to react with water. They do react, but it takes a bit longer to see what is happening.

 7 If you leave an iron nail in water, what evidence will there be after a week that a chemical reaction has taken place?

We now have enough information to place the metals in a league table based on their **reactivity**. We call this league table the **reactivity series**. If we know their position in the reactivity series, we can use it to **predict** how other metals will behave.

 8 Nickel is a metal that is a little more reactive than copper but not as reactive as iron.

    a How will nickel behave when you put it in water?

    b Colette thinks we could use nickel to make coins. Do you agree? Explain your answer.

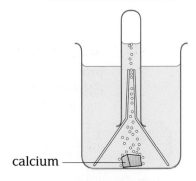

Calcium and magnesium both react with water to produce bubbles of hydrogen.

calcium

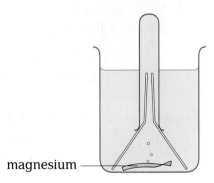

magnesium

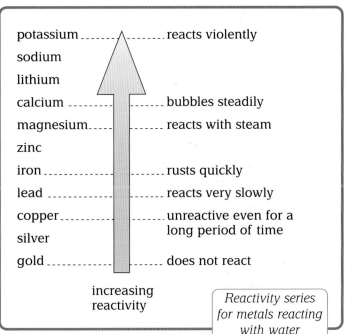

potassium · · · · · · · · · · reacts violently
sodium
lithium
calcium · · · · · · · · · · · bubbles steadily
magnesium · · · · · · · · · reacts with steam
zinc
iron · · · · · · · · · · · · · rusts quickly
lead · · · · · · · · · · · · · reacts very slowly
copper · · · · · · · · · · · unreactive even for a
                   long period of time
silver
gold · · · · · · · · · · · · · does not react

increasing
reactivity

Reactivity series for metals reacting with water

9F.3 Reactivity of metals with acids

Only a few metals react quickly with water. The reaction between metals and acids is much more vigorous. When a metal does react with an acid, it is easy to see that a reaction is happening. Bubbles of gas are produced and the metal gradually disappears. The metal reacts with the acid to a form a new substance that is soluble in water. The gas produced is hydrogen and the other new substance is a **salt**. Most salts are soluble in water.

We can also look at the number of bubbles of hydrogen that are produced when reacting metals with cold or hot acid. Less reactive metals react only with hot acid.

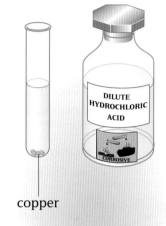
copper

 1   From the diagrams, what is the evidence that copper is more reactive than gold?

 2   Look at the diagrams at the bottom of the page. Which metal:

   a reacts fastest with cold acid;

   b reacts the most slowly with hot acid?

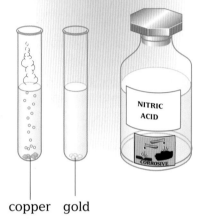
copper   gold

 3   Based on their reactions with cold acid and hot acid, place these four metals in order of reactivity.

4   Which metal is the most difficult to place in order? Explain your answer.

The reactivity series for the reactions between acids and metals is very similar to the one for water. But we get more detailed information because more metals react with acid than with water.

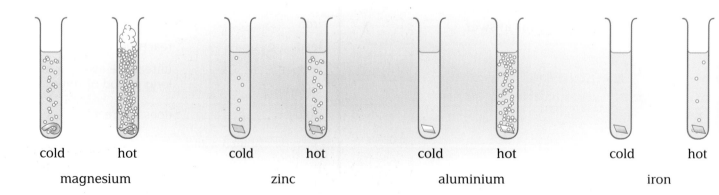

cold	hot	cold	hot	cold	hot	cold	hot
magnesium		zinc		aluminium		iron	

9F.4 Metals and oxygen

The reaction between metals and oxygen is important because all the metals that we use every day are exposed to the oxygen in the atmosphere.

For example, steel is used to make cars, bridges and railway lines. Steel is made from iron, a moderately reactive metal. It reacts with oxygen to make iron oxide which is much weaker than iron. So the iron gradually reacts with oxygen and loses its strength.

One way to protect metals is to paint them.

 1 Why do we not make bridges and cars out of gold, silver or copper? Give at least <u>two</u> reasons.

The word equation for the reaction between iron and oxygen is:

iron + oxygen → iron oxide

There is also water vapour in the atmosphere. Iron reacts with both water and oxygen to produce a substance called hydrated iron oxide. We usually call it 'rust'.

The word equation for rusting is:

iron + water + oxygen → hydrated iron oxide
(rust)

We protect iron objects such as cars and bridges against rusting by preventing oxygen and water from getting to the metal.

Another way to protect metals is to oil them.

 2 How do we protect bridges and cars from rusting?

 3 Write word equations for the following reactions:
  a copper and oxygen;
  b magnesium and oxygen;
  c sodium and oxygen.

Magnesium burns very brightly.

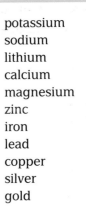

potassium
sodium
lithium
calcium
magnesium
zinc
iron
lead
copper
silver
gold

increasing reactivity with oxygen

Again, we can make a reactivity series and use it to make predictions about other metals.

9F.5 Displacement reactions

Reactive metals tend not to remain as pure metals but to combine with other elements to form compounds.

As you have seen, the most reactive metals, such as potassium and sodium, react the most quickly.

When two metals are present, they compete to form new compounds. The more reactive metal will win the competition. We call a competition reaction a **displacement reaction**.

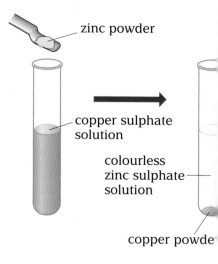

zinc powder

copper sulphate solution

colourless zinc sulphate solution

copper powder

1 What evidence is there of a chemical reaction between the zinc powder and the copper sulphate solution?

2 Describe the <u>two</u> products of the reaction between copper sulphate and zinc.

The word equation for this reaction is:

zinc + copper sulphate → zinc sulphate + copper
metal   solution   solution   metal

Copper sulphate and zinc sulphate are salts. Zinc is a more reactive metal than copper, so it **displaces** the copper from the copper sulphate and forms its own salt, zinc sulphate. The displaced copper is no longer part of a compound. It is an element – the orange/brown metal at the bottom of the test-tube.

3 Why does the liquid in the test-tube change from blue to colourless?

If you put a strip of copper metal into zinc sulphate solution, nothing happens. This is because the copper is the less reactive of the two and therefore cannot displace the zinc.

You can use the results of reactions between metals and solutions of metal salts to work out whether one metal is more reactive than another.

4 Look at the results of the experiments. In which of the experiments is there evidence of a chemical reaction?

5 Use these results to place the metals in an order of reactivity.

At the start	A few minutes later
copper / tin nitrate	tin nitrate
copper / magnesium nitrate	magnesium nitrate
tin / copper nitrate	tin crystals
tin / magnesium nitrate	magnesium nitrate
magnesium / copper nitrate	copper crystals
magnesium / tin nitrate	tin crystals

We can think of displacement reactions as a 'trial of strength' to see which metal will win the battle and become part of a salt rather than stay as a pure metal.

- Reactive metals, such as potassium and sodium, are really strong and will win most battles.

- Unreactive metals, such as copper and silver, are weak and usually lose their battles.

- Moderately reactive metals, such as iron or zinc, are somewhere in the middle and therefore they win some battles and lose others.

6 Which metal do you think will win the following battles, based on their position in the reactivity series?

   a magnesium and iron

   b gold and silver

   c zinc and copper

   d sodium and calcium

   e zinc and iron

   f potassium and sodium

A useful displacement reaction

In reactions between a metal and a metal oxide, the more reactive metal takes oxygen away from the less reactive metal. We say that it **displaces** the less reactive metal. The Thermit reaction uses this difference in reactivity between two metals, aluminium and iron. We use it to produce molten iron to repair railway lines on site. The Thermit mixture contains iron oxide and aluminium. When the mixture is heated, the more reactive aluminium takes the oxygen away from the iron oxide to produce pure iron. The heat given off in the reaction is so intense that it makes the iron melt.

The word equation for this reaction is:

iron oxide + aluminium → aluminium oxide + iron

7 Which of the substances in the equation are:

a elements;

b compounds?

8 When iron is mixed with aluminium oxide and then heated, there is no reaction. Explain why.

9 In which of the following mixtures will heating result in a chemical reaction?

- copper and magnesium oxide
- magnesium and copper oxide
- magnesium and iron oxide
- zinc and copper oxide
- zinc and magnesium oxide

9F.6 Sources and uses of metals

Only a few metals are found in their natural state. We call them 'native' metals. Examples are gold, silver and copper.

1 Where are gold, silver and copper in the reactivity series?

Gold, silver and copper were the first metals people ever used because they were easy to extract from the ground. All people had to do was:

- separate the metal from the rocks around it;
- heat up the metal until it melted;
- mould the metal to form the shape they wanted.

Although these metals were better than the stone and wood that had been used before, they were not good enough for some jobs.

2 Look at the cartoon. Suggest why copper and gold were not always the best metals for the job.

The search has been on ever since to find more useful metals, but that is not as easy as it sounds. Most metals are found chemically combined with other elements such as oxygen and sulphur. The rocks that contain these compounds are called **ores**. **Haematite** is an ore containing a compound of iron called iron oxide (Fe_2O_3).

3 How do you think the metals in rocks ended up chemically joined to oxygen?

Rock salt is mostly sodium combined with chlorine.

Bauxite is an ore that we get aluminium from. It is mainly aluminium combined with oxygen.

Galena is an ore that we get lead from. It is mainly lead combined with sulphur.

Haematite is an ore that we get iron from. It is mainly iron combined with oxygen.

4 How many elements are present in the compound iron oxide?

5 What is the name of aluminium ore?

6 Which metal is found in rock salt?

7 What is the name of an ore from which we can extract lead?

Before we can use these metals, we have to extract them from their ores. In the case of the iron oxide, we need to separate the iron from the oxygen in the compound. About 3500 years ago, people discovered that they could extract iron from its ore by heating it with charcoal using a very hot flame. Heating with charcoal can be used to extract lead, zinc and tin too.

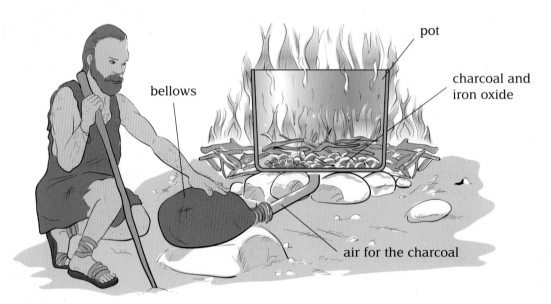

pot

charcoal and iron oxide

bellows

air for the charcoal

8 Look back at page 113. Where in the reactivity series are the metals that can be extracted using charcoal?

Nowadays we extract iron in a blast furnace. The diagram shows what happens.

iron ore (iron oxide)   coke (carbon)

waste gases out

air
iron oxide → ← waste gases
reaction
carbon → ← iron

Oxygen is taken away from the iron oxide; iron is left behind.

The furnace is so hot that the iron melts.

blast of hot air

molten iron

Molten iron is run off.

9 What is blown into the blast furnace?

10 What is the source of the carbon?

11 How do you get the iron out of the blast furnace?

By 1800 only 12 metals were in common use. Only unreactive metals could be fairly extracted using carbon (charcoal), or hydrogen. More reactive metals, such as aluminium, magnesium and sodium, will not give up their oxygen to carbon or to hydrogen.

In 1807, the scientist Humphry Davy invented a new method of extracting very reactive metals. In an experiment he passed an electric current through a sample of moistened potash (a compound of potassium) on a platinum dish. He noticed that small globules of metal collected around the negative electrode. The metal that collected was potassium. He extracted sodium in a similar way.

This method of extracting metals by using an electric current is called **electrolysis**. Soon scientists found out how to use this method to extract metals such as calcium, barium, magnesium and aluminium. At first this method of extraction was very expensive. Napoleon III (1808–1873), the emperor of France, had a special dinner service made of aluminium which he used on special occasions to impress guests. Eventually the cost of these metals was reduced as scientists improved the methods of extraction. Aluminium is now a relatively cheap metal.

Humphry Davy (1778–1829).

Alloy	Metals in them
bronze	copper and tin
brass	copper and zinc
pewter	lead and tin
steel	iron and carbon

12 What is aluminium oxide split up into?

13 Name <u>two</u> examples of household uses of aluminium which show that it must be relatively cheap.

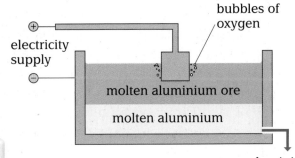

bubbles of oxygen

electricity supply

molten aluminium ore

molten aluminium

aluminium out

We extract aluminium by melting aluminium oxide and passing electricity through it.

By the end of the 19th century another 41 metals had been extracted from their ores. The Industrial Revolution depended on the availability of various metals that could do different jobs and could be produced economically. Look at the table.

Metal	Date of first extraction	Use
gold	6000 BC	jewellery
copper	4200 BC	electrical wiring
iron	1500 BC	railway lines
sodium	1807	street lighting
aluminium	1827	overhead cables

14 a Why is gold used for jewellery?

   b Why can aluminium be used for overhead cables?

   c Why can iron be used for railway lines?

9F.7 Investigating metals and acids further

Joy and Dan are investigating the reactivity of different metals with hydrochloric acid. When three of these metals react with acid, bubbles of gas are produced.

1 What is the name of the gas produced?

The other product is a salt. When you use hydrochloric acid, the salt produced is always a chloride. So when magnesium reacts with hydrochloric acid, the salt produced is magnesium chloride.

2 What are the products when aluminium reacts with hydrochloric acid?

Joy thinks that they can compare the reactivity of metals by looking at the number of bubbles produced when you add a strip of metal to some hydrochloric acid.

3 What must Joy do to make sure this a fair test?
4 Look at the diagram. Then place the metals in an order of reactivity.

Two of the metals give very similar results. Joy decides that measuring the volume of gas produced would be more accurate than counting bubbles. She collects the gas in a burette.

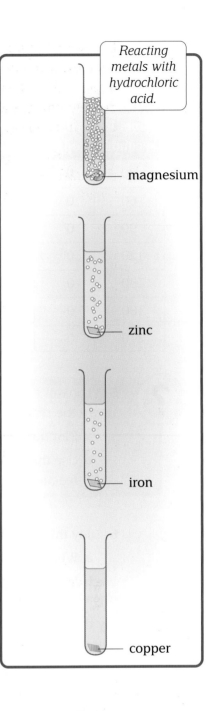

Reacting metals with hydrochloric acid.

— magnesium

— zinc

— iron

— copper

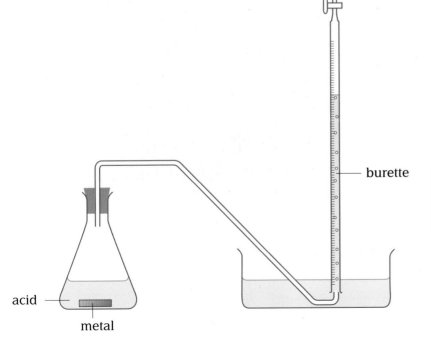

— burette

— acid

— metal

The hydrogen produced pushes the water out of the burette.

Joy carried out this improved experiment and got the following results.

Time, in seconds	Volume of gas produced, in cm³			
	with copper	with magnesium	with iron	with zinc
30	0	4.0	1.0	1.5
60	0	8.0	3.0	3.0
90	0	13.0	5.0	6.0
120	0	18.0	7.0	9.0
150	0	22.5	9.0	12.0
180	0	26.0	10.5	14.0
210	0	28.0	11.5	15.5

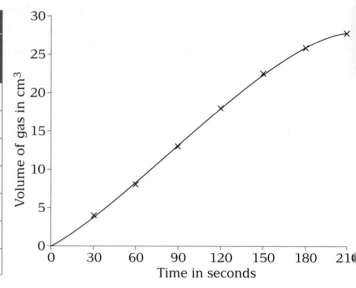

This graph shows the volume of hydrogen produced in the reaction with magnesium.

5 Look at the graph of the volume of hydrogen produced in the reaction with magnesium.

 a Plot a similar graph for iron and zinc;

 b Use these graphs to place the metals in order of reactivity.

6 Joy thinks that magnesium is twice as reactive as zinc.

 a What is her evidence?

 b Do you agree with her conclusion? Explain your answer.

Joy then decides that she will use this method to compare these four metals with another metal – aluminium.

7 Based on its position in the reactivity series, what results would <u>you</u> expect for aluminium?

8 Do these results match your prediction? Explain your answer.

These are Joy's results for aluminium.

Time in seconds	Volume in cm³
30	0.5
60	1.0
90	1.5
120	2.0
150	4.0
180	7.0
210	10.0

You should now understand the key words
and key ideas shown below.

- Metals will gradually react with the air and water from the atmosphere.
- Copper and gold will not **tarnish** even after a long time.
- Sodium and potassium tarnish so quickly that they need to be stored in oil.
- Sodium and potassium are **alkali metals**. They are soft and easy to cut.

- Some metals react with cold water to produce hydrogen.
- Some metals react more readily with water than others.

- Metals react with acids to produce hydrogen and a **salt**.
- Some metals react more readily with acids than others.
- Some metals do not react with acids.

- Metals react with oxygen to form oxides.
- The **reactivity series** for metals with oxygen is generally similar to that for water and acids.

- In a **displacement reaction,** a metal **displaces** a less reactive metal from a solution of one of its salts.
- We can use the order of **reactivity** of metals to make **predictions** about other metals that have not been observed.

- Metals have a variety of different uses.

- The reactivity of a metal affects its uses and the extraction method from its **ore**:
  - Less reactive metals such as iron are extracted by reacting the ore with carbon. The way iron is extracted from **haematite**.
  - Reactive metals such as sodium need to be extracted by **electrolysis**.

Environmental chemistry

In this unit we shall be studying some of the ways in which humans have polluted the world. We shall consider the evidence for acid rain and for global warming.

KEY WORDS
vegetation cover
acid rain
corrosion
catalytic converter
reliable
insufficient data
monitoring
air quality
indicator organisms
biased
global warming
greenhouse effect
climate change

9G.1 Are soils different from each other?

Soil is not the same all over the world. There are clay soils, sandy soils and chalky soils; there are dry soils and sticky soils. Local rocks, plants and soil animals all affect what the soil is like.

Weathering and erosion of rocks produce smaller pieces that become part of the soil. Dead plant and animal matter add humus to soil. As the humus breaks down further, it adds mineral nutrients to the soil. The amount of plant growth – also called **vegetation cover** – is therefore very important in the formation of soil. Soil animals make burrows that help air get into the soil. Plant roots need oxygen from the air.

These soil crumbs contain tiny bits of broken rock and animal and plant matter.

Gardeners dig compost and manure into soil. Compost is rotted plant material.

Earthworms make burrows that help air get into the soil.

1 Look at the photographs. How do earthworms and compost affect soil?

Some soils are good for lots of types of plants, some are good for a only a few types of plants, and others are no good for plants at all. One important factor in this is the acidity of the soil. Most plants grow best in soil that has a pH of between 6 and 8.

2 Find out what:

    a the pH scale measures;

    b pH 6 means;

    c pH 7 means;

    d pH 8 means.

Some plants grow well in soil that is acidic, other plants grow well in soil that is alkaline. The table gives some examples.

Plants for acidic soils	Plants for alkaline soils
crocus	cowslip
rhododendron	lilac
camellia	flowering cherry
chinese witch hazel	wallflower
good-luck plant	iris

3 Look at the photographs. Which garden has soil that is alkaline and which garden has soil that is acidic? Explain your answers.

4 What would you say to a gardener who wanted to grow rhododendrons and cowslips side-by-side?

Neutralising acid soils

Lots of farms and gardens have soils that are too acidic for many plants. We make these soils less acidic by adding powdered limestone or other forms of lime to neutralise some of the acid. Limestone is a naturally occurring form of calcium carbonate. It is cheap and plentiful in the UK.

5 Find out how farmers or gardeners test soil to see what its pH is.

6 What do scientists mean by <u>neutralise</u>?

Cowslips and a rhododendron bush growing in two different gardens.

9G.2 Acid rain

Acid rain falling on us sounds <u>really</u> nasty! It suggests that the rain will burn holes in our coats, burn away our skin and kill all the grass. We need to know some more about acid rain before we make up our minds.

A scientist goes to Ascension Island, which is in the middle of the Atlantic Ocean. It is a long way away from any pollution so the rain should be pure and clean. When the scientist collects some rainwater and tests it with universal indicator, the indicator turns yellow! This means its pH is about 5.5 – the rain is a weak acid. The conclusion is that <u>unpolluted</u> rain is acidic. Acidic rain is natural.

1   What does the test result tell us about the rain on Ascension Island?

2   What does <u>unpolluted</u> mean?

The scientist leaves Ascension Island and tests rainwater from Faxton, a town in a busy industrial part of England. This time the universal indicator turns orange. The pH of the rain is about 4. Something has made the rain more acidic than the rain on Ascension Island. The rain from Faxton has been <u>polluted</u>. This is what we mean by acid rain – rainwater with an <u>unusually</u> low pH due to pollution.

3   What does the test result tell us about the rain in Faxton?

4   What does <u>polluted</u> mean?

5   How is the rain in Faxton different from the rain in Ascension Island? Suggest a reason for the difference.

What does acid rain do to rocks and building materials?

The table shows what happens to some different kinds of rock when you add them to dilute acid.

Example of rock	What happens to the rock in acid
granite	little or no change
sandstone with a silica cement	little or no change
sandstone with a carbonate cement	falls apart as the cement reacts with the acid
limestone	fizzes and disappears
chalk	fizzes and disappears

6   What does acid do to chalk and limestone?

7   What does acid do to sandstone with a carbonate cement?

8   Explain what happens to sandstone with a carbonate cement in acid.

9   The rocks in the table are all building materials. Which <u>two</u> rocks would be best to use in Faxton? Explain your answer.

10 The statue has been eaten away by acid rain. What type of rock could it be made from?

Does anything else affect rocks in this way?

When something gets worn away we say that it is <u>weathered</u>. We see this happening to the rocks out in the countryside and to the building materials our homes are made of. It is not only acid rain that weathers rocks.

- <u>Plant roots</u> break tiny bits off rocks as they force their way into tiny cracks. The cracks get bigger and the rock breaks.

- <u>Rivers</u> gradually wear away the rocks on their riverbeds.

- In the winter, <u>water</u> in cracks in rocks freezes and expands. The rocks crack and bits break off when the ice melts.

- <u>Our feet</u> wear away rocks and paths as we walk over them.

All these changes are very slow, but they do happen.

11 How did the Grand Canyon form?

12 What wore away the steps?

13 What broke up the paving slabs?

Acid rain affects some metals

Acids also eat away some metals. This is called **corrosion**.

Acid rain is <u>very</u> dilute, but it has still corroded these metal railings faster than normal rain.

LEAD   IRON   ZINC

You can see the bubbles of hydrogen produced as metals react with acid. Notice that the lead is not reacting.

14 Which metal corrodes the fastest?

15 Which metal would you use to make a tank for holding acid? Explain your answer.

16 Why does it take a long time for metal railings to rust away?

What does acid rain do to plants?

Trees and other plants can survive the slight amount of acid that is naturally in rain, but the extra acidity caused by pollution can slowly kill them. The more acidic the rain, the faster minerals drain out of the soil. Some plants cannot survive the extra acidity and the shortage of minerals.

This tree's needles are falling off and it is dying! This is because it is growing in an area where the rain is very acidic.

17 Look at the picture of the tree. In what ways does it look unhealthy?

What does acid rain do to animals?

Polluted rain has a pH of around 4. Humans can happily drink orange juice and cola, both of which are more acidic than this. Acid rain doesn't have much effect on large animals like us.

18 Which is more acidic, polluted rain or cola?

Frogs, fish and other types of water life have a much bigger problem, however. All the rain drains into the lakes and rivers where they live. They can't get away from the acid.

- The acid stops the water creatures' eggs from hatching and it kills the young fish and tadpoles soon after they have hatched.
- Acid kills the water plants and insects that the older fish eat, and then the fish starve.
- Acidic water draining off the land carries extra aluminium, which stops a fish's gills working properly.

This gradual reduction in the number and variety of living things is called <u>progressive depletion</u>. The smaller and more acid-sensitive creatures disappear first. But, in the end, all the living things disappear.

There is nothing alive in this river.

19 Why does nothing live in the river?
Suggest at least <u>two</u> possible reasons.

9G.3 What causes acid rain?

The photographs all show things that help to cause acid rain. They are all putting one or more gases that can make acidic solutions into the air! Yes, Paul Scholes is doing this, not just when he plays football, but every time he breathes out. These gases mix in with the rest of the atmosphere, near the ground and high in the air. As rain falls through the air some of the gases dissolve. This makes the rain more acidic.

1 Name <u>four</u> things that put gases that make acidic rain into the air.
2 How do these four things give out these gases?
3 How do the gases make the rain acidic?

4 Why is the rain acidic even if you live far away from any industrial pollution?

All living things give out carbon dioxide. Volcanoes give out carbon dioxide and sulphur dioxide. Sulphur dioxide dissolves in rain to make a strong acid.

Cars, lorries and aircraft give out carbon dioxide, sulphur dioxide and nitrogen oxides. Nitrogen oxides dissolve in rain to make a strong acid. Power station chimneys give out carbon dioxide and sulphur dioxide. The atmosphere contains over 3 billion tonnes of carbon dioxide. It dissolves in water to form a very weak acid.

 5 Identify all the sources of gases that make acid rain in the picture.

6 Which sources of these gases are natural and which are artificial?

7 Which of these gases does each source give out?

 8 Which of these gases dissolve to form strong acids?

 9 Trees are a source of carbon dioxide because they give out carbon dioxide at night. However, they use carbon dioxide during the day. In a typical 24-hour period, do trees make more carbon dioxide than they use, or not? Explain your answer.

9G.4 Can we reduce the amount of acid in the rain?

Human beings can be lazy and greedy! Our cars and industries release a lot of gases that can dissolve to form acid rain into the air, and we have done little to stop this, or even to reduce it. We could:

- use more renewable energy sources;
- burn less fuel;
- remove the sulphur from fossil fuels before we burn them;
- remove the gases from chimney smoke and car exhaust fumes.

All these things take effort and cost money. But we must do it – there is only one Earth; when we pollute it, we still have to live on it.

 1 Why have people done so little about reducing pollution?

 2 Why is it important to reduce pollution?

Making car exhausts cleaner

The gases that come out of the exhaust pipe of a car are called its <u>emissions</u>. These emissions include nitrogen oxides, sulphur dioxide and carbon monoxide. Carbon monoxide is the gas that makes car exhaust fumes so poisonous.

We can use **catalytic converters** to make the nitrogen oxide gases react with the carbon monoxide gas in the exhaust.

nitrogen oxides + carbon monoxide → nitrogen + carbon dioxide

Inside the catalytic converter the substance that does this job is called the <u>catalyst</u>. The catalyst slowly gets dirty and this stops it from working, so occasionally it has to be replaced. A replacement costs around £300, so it is not cheap.

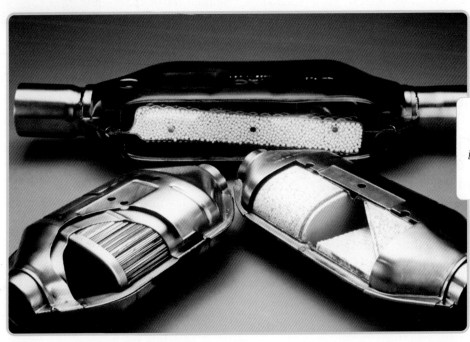

The catalytic converter is in the car's exhaust system. Catalysts on special surfaces inside the converter speed up the reactions that make the exhaust gases less polluting.

3   Why are nitrogen oxides bad for the environment?

4   Why is carbon monoxide dangerous?

5   Where is a catalytic converter fitted on a car?

6   What does a catalytic converter do?

7   Why do catalytic converters need to be replaced sometimes?

8   Why might a car owner not be pleased about having to replace the catalytic converter?

9   By law, all new cars in the UK must have a catalytic converter. Make a guess of how many cars there are in the street where you live. Now work out the cost of fitting a catalytic converter to all of them.

Catalytic converters cannot reduce the amount of sulphur dioxide in the exhaust emissions. That is why low sulphur petrol was developed. There is still some sulphur in the petrol though, and this causes the familiar 'eggy' smell from the exhaust when a car hasn't quite warmed up.

10 How does using low sulphur petrol help to prevent acid rain?

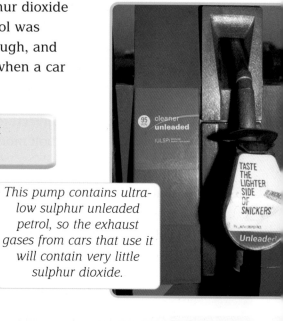

The gases that come out of the chimneys of a power station are also called emissions. These emissions include sulphur dioxide. It is possible to remove the sulphur dioxide, but it is expensive.

This pump contains ultra-low sulphur unleaded petrol, so the exhaust gases from cars that use it will contain very little sulphur dioxide.

Air quality

Scientists need to know whether or not air pollution is getting worse. First, they must collect information. This information is called <u>data</u>. It must be collected accurately and carefully, so that it can be relied on. Enough data must be collected for the scientists to be sure that it reflects general trends. Otherwise, the data could be just the records of a few days of unusual air pollution. Data that is collected accurately, carefully and in a sufficient amount is said to be **reliable**. If the scientists don't have enough data for making a good decision, they say they have **insufficient data**.

Scientists measure the amounts of pollutants in the air every day. We call this **monitoring** the **air quality**. To 'monitor' something means to measure it regularly, so that any changes will be detected.

	low	moderate	high	very high
index	(1-3)	(4-6)	(7-9)	(10)
sulphur dioxide (ppb)	less than 100	100–199	200–399	400+
ozone (ppb)	less than 50	50–89	80–179	180+
carbon monoxide (ppm)	less than 10	10–14	15–19	20+
nitrogen dioxide (ppb)	less than 150	150–299	300–399	400+
particles(PM$_{10}$) (mcg per m^{-3})	less than 50	50–74	75–99	100+

UK Department of the Environment standard for air quality

	London	Leeds	Hull
sulphur dioxide (ppb)	50	44	57
ozone (ppb)	14	15	30
carbon monoxide (ppm)	11	9	6
nitrogen dioxide (ppb)	38	16	8
particles(PM$_{10}$) (mcg per m^{-3})	22	16	24

Data for April 1

11 What is the difference between <u>testing</u> air quality and <u>monitoring</u> it?

12 Which air pollutants do local authorities monitor?

13 Why do local authorities put air quality tables in local newspapers?

Air quality tables are published in newspapers. Sometimes people with breathing problems are warned to stay indoors as much as possible.

One way to monitor air quality is to use pumps to suck air through special tubes called <u>sorbent tubes</u>. These tubes contain filters and chemicals. The chemicals in the tubes trap pollutant gases, such as the gases that cause acid rain. The filters trap the smoke and soot particles that come from vehicle exhausts and chimneys. These particles can irritate our lungs and throats, and cause bronchitis and asthma to get worse.

By analysing the filters and chemicals in the tubes every day, scientists know how much of each pollutant there is. Rain is monitored too. Scientists put rain gauges (also called rain collectors) in open spaces all over the world. Each rain gauge is checked every day. Scientists can tell from the amount of water in the gauge how much rain has fallen during the day. By analysing the water they can find out how acidic the rain is and whether or not it contains other pollutants too.

We can also learn about air quality in a particular area by monitoring the plant life. Some plant species can only grow in clean air. We call these species **indicator organisms**.

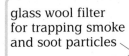

glass wool filter for trapping smoke and soot particles

layers of chemicals to trap pollutant gases from the air

This sort of tube is called a sorbent tube. It is used for monitoring air quality.

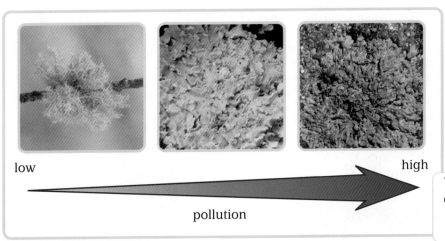

low

high

pollution

The cleaner the air, the more species of lichens there are. Shrubby lichens grow only in air with very low concentrations of sulphur dioxide.

14 Do you think that the number of species of lichens would <u>increase</u> or <u>decrease</u> as you go out from a city centre? Give reasons for your answer.

15 In a churchyard near a power station, there are no lichens growing on the gravestones. The leaves on a sycamore tree have no tar spots on them.

  a What does this suggest about the air quality in the churchyard?

  b What could be affecting the air quality?

  c Do you think the churchyard gives the scientist sufficient data to come to a definite conclusion?

The 'tar spots' on these sycamore leaves are caused by a fungus that grows only where the air is clean.

Through monitoring our air and rain quality, we can state, without guesswork, whether the air pollution is increasing, staying the same, or decreasing. We can decide whether or not our actions to reduce pollution are working.

It would not be right to leave all the monitoring to the people who run power stations and factories and to the car makers. It is possible that they might be biased. To be **biased** means to present facts or draw conclusions in a way that suits you or your organisation, rather than telling the strict truth.

16 Car manufacturers might be biased in reporting how clean their cars' exhausts are. Suggest reasons for this.

Photographic and historical evidence

We can also learn about the changing nature of air and rain quality from old photographs and books, or even just by looking around.

In 2000 there was a lot of scaffolding on Lincoln Cathedral whilst repairs were made to stonework damaged by acid rain.

This photograph of Lincoln Cathedral taken in 1900 shows a building that has suffered very little damage from air pollution in six hundred years. The statues and carved stones still looked detailed and beautiful.

Written records can also teach us much. Life in Widnes in Victorian times must have been grim. Historical accounts say there was not one green leaf or blade of grass in the town. We believe that this was due to emissions from the local chemical industry, which caused the rain there to be <u>pH 1</u>. Nowadays, Widnes is a normal town, with gardens and parks.

These chemical workers in Widnes wore goggles and had every scrap of skin covered to protect them from the acidic gases produced by the industry they worked in.

17 Explain how the photographs and their captions provide evidence that pollution has got better in one place but has got worse in another place.

9G.5 Is global warming really happening?

The data collected on air temperatures, wind and rainfall has enabled scientists to come to a startling conclusion. This conclusion is that the average temperature of the Earth is higher now than it was 100 years ago. The increase in temperature of just over 0.5 °C doesn't sound much. However, most of this increase has happened in the last 20 years. Some scientists fear that the average surface temperature of the Earth could rise by up to 5 °C by the year 2100. They call it **global warming** and it would be serious.

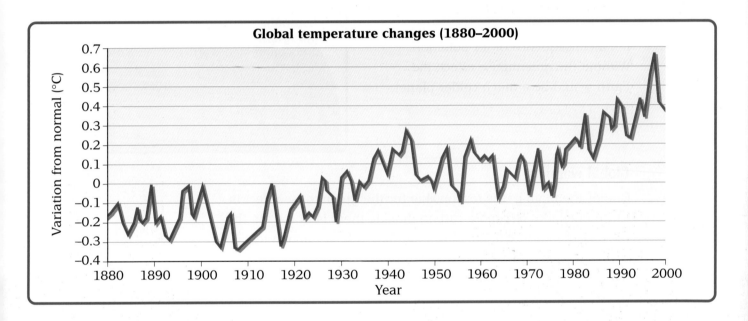

Global temperature changes (1880–2000)

1   By how much could the average surface temperature of the Earth rise by the year 2100?

2   Look at the graph.

   a What general trend does the graph show?

   b Find a 50-year period during which the temperature trend hardly changed.

   c Find a 30-year period during which the temperature trend went down slightly.

   d Find the 20-year period during which the temperature trend went up the most.

The greenhouse effect

The Sun's rays continually heat the Earth. Fortunately, the Earth doesn't just get hotter and hotter because it also radiates heat back into space. Some gases in the atmosphere reduce this heat loss. The gases trap heat like a duvet on a bed or the glass in a greenhouse, with the result that the average temperature of the Earth stays more or less the same. This is called the **greenhouse effect**. The greenhouse effect is a <u>natural</u> effect, not a consequence of air pollution. Without the greenhouse effect, the Earth would be a much colder planet.

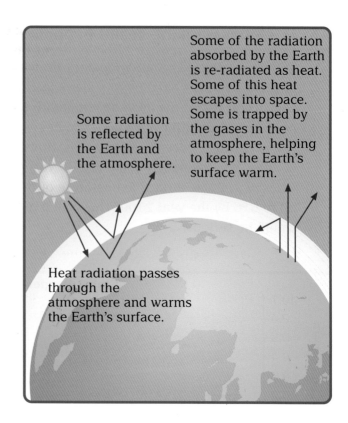

Some radiation is reflected by the Earth and the atmosphere.

Some of the radiation absorbed by the Earth is re-radiated as heat. Some of this heat escapes into space. Some is trapped by the gases in the atmosphere, helping to keep the Earth's surface warm.

Heat radiation passes through the atmosphere and warms the Earth's surface.

Global warming

One of the main gases responsible for the greenhouse effect is carbon dioxide. The more carbon dioxide there is in the air, the warmer the Earth will be. Before human industry began to pollute the air, the Earth's atmosphere had been in a finely balanced position for millions of years. Photosynthesis by plants used up carbon dioxide, and respiration by plants and animals made carbon dioxide. The amount of carbon dioxide stayed constant at around 0.03% of the air. This was just enough to cause a greenhouse effect that kept the Earth at a suitable temperature for the life on the planet. It was like a perfect duvet, one you would never want to change.

3   Is the greenhouse effect natural or caused by humans?

4   **a** Name <u>one</u> gas responsible for the greenhouse effect.

    b State <u>one</u> natural process that uses up this gas and <u>one</u> natural process that makes this gas.

If you put a thicker duvet on your bed tonight you would be warmer – possibly even too hot. In a similar way, as we increase the amount of carbon dioxide in the atmosphere, the Earth gets warmer. Nearly all scientists believe that global warming is happening and that the extra carbon dioxide is the cause.

Our lives at home and the successful working of the industries that make our goods and possessions rely on electricity. Worldwide, most electricity is generated in power stations that burn fossil fuels – coal, oil and gas. Our road transport uses petrol or diesel, and jet aircraft burn kerosene. All of these fossil fuels contain carbon, so when they burn they release carbon dioxide. Our increasing use of fossil fuels for making electricity and for transport explains why carbon dioxide levels are rising.

Might climate change mean this?

5 Explain <u>two</u> ways that human activity increases the amount of carbon dioxide in the air.

As the world warms up, weather patterns everywhere will change. This is called **climate change**. Not everyone agrees about exactly how weather patterns will change. For parts of the world this will be pleasant. Some people think that the climate in the UK might become more like that of Spain. Elsewhere the changes will not be welcome. Great deserts, such as the Sahara, could increase in size and eventually cover much land that is fertile today. As the oceans warm up they will expand. This effect, along with water released by melting ice caps, will cause sea levels to rise, flooding low-lying land around the world. The worst predictions are that over 75% of land in England would flood permanently. Wales, Scotland and Ireland would keep a higher percentage of dry land, as they are more hilly.

or this?

6 What effect of global warming does each cartoon illustrate?

The scientists of the world do not all agree on whether or not increased amounts of carbon dioxide are causing global warming. They <u>do</u> agree that global warming <u>is</u> happening, but some claim that it is part of a natural cycle of an ice age followed by a warming up period, then another ice age, and so on. These scientists believe we are in the warming up period following the ice age that ended 11 000 years ago. However, 9 out of 10 weather scientists believe that global warming is caused by increased amounts of carbon dioxide.

or this?

7 What are the <u>two</u> possible causes of global warming?
8 What percentage of weather scientists believe in each of the possible causes?

You should now understand the key words and key ideas shown below.

Key words
vegetation cover
acid rain
corrosion
catalytic converter
reliable
insufficient data
monitoring
air quality
indicator organisms
biased
global warming
greenhouse effect
climate change

KEY IDEAS

- Rocks and building materials are slowly weathered and eroded.

- Soil forms from the interactions between rock fragments and living things.

- Different soils can have different pH values, making them suitable for different plants.

- Acidic soils can be made less acidic by adding lime.

- Rain is naturally slightly acidic due to dissolved carbon dioxide.

- Nitrogen oxides and sulphur dioxide gases are produced by human industrial activity. They increase the acidity of rain.

- As rain becomes more acidic, the weathering and erosion of rocks and building materials speeds up.

- Acid rain corrodes some metals, and is damaging to some life forms.

- The use of low sulphur petrol and catalytic converters in cars can reduce the emissions that cause acid rain.

- Air and water quality are closely monitored and measured.

- The Earth's atmosphere reduces heat loss into space. This is the greenhouse effect.

- The Earth's climate is getting warmer. We call this global warming.

- Global warming is probably due to increased amounts of carbon dioxide in the atmosphere.

Using chemistry

In this unit we shall be finding out more about using chemicals as an energy source and seeing how to make new materials. We shall use word equations and symbol equations to represent chemical reactions. We shall also discover how atoms are rearranged, but not lost or made, during a chemical reaction.

KEY WORDS
hydrocarbon
incomplete combustion
oxidation
cell
electrochemical series
trial
law of conservation
  of mass
phlogiston

9H.1 What chemical reactions take place when fuels burn?

In Units 7F and 9F you saw how burning chemicals is called <u>combustion</u>. Combustion does not always involve flames, smoke and sparks. It involves a rapid reaction with oxygen from the air to make new substances, called oxides. Oxides are compounds that contain oxygen and one other element.

1   Name <u>three</u> oxides you have seen in earlier science work.

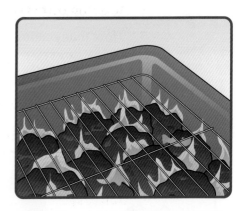

Combustion and oxides

When we burn a substance, the oxygen from the air reacts with elements and compounds in the substance to form oxides. Sometimes this is difficult to see because the reactions involve colourless gases such as oxygen and carbon dioxide.

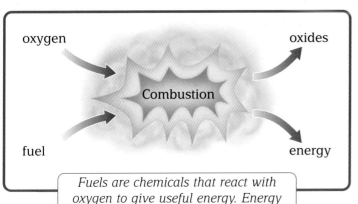

Fuels are chemicals that react with oxygen to give useful energy. Energy is always released when a fuel burns.

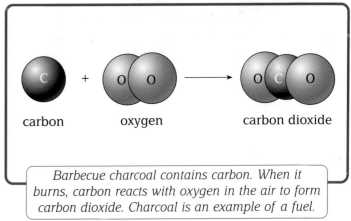

Barbecue charcoal contains carbon. When it burns, carbon reacts with oxygen in the air to form carbon dioxide. Charcoal is an example of a fuel.

2 Name the substances formed when:

   a iron burns;

   b hydrogen undergoes combustion.

3 Write down a process in the human body that is similar to combustion.

The gas that is used in gas cookers and in Bunsen burners is called natural gas. Its chemical name is methane. It belongs to a group of compounds called **hydrocarbons**. Hydrocarbons contain hydrogen and carbon only.

We get natural gas from rocks below the surface of the North Sea.

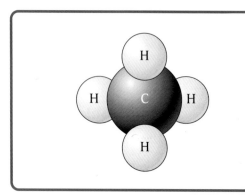

A molecule of methane contains one carbon atom and four hydrogen atoms. It has the formula CH_4.

4 What type of compound is methane?

5 How many atoms does a methane molecule contain?

We can write an equation for the combustion of methane:

methane + oxygen → carbon dioxide + hydrogen oxide (water) + energy

$$CH_4 + 2O_2 \rightarrow CO_2 + 2H_2O + energy$$

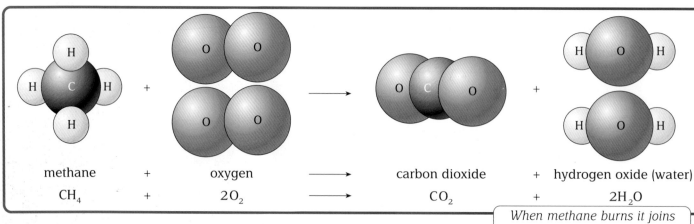

| methane | + | oxygen | ⟶ | carbon dioxide | + | hydrogen oxide (water) |
| CH_4 | + | $2O_2$ | ⟶ | CO_2 | + | $2H_2O$ |

When methane burns it joins up with oxygen in the air to form the oxides carbon dioxide and water.

6 How many molecules of water are made when one molecule of methane is burnt completely?

Not completely burnt

Sometimes there is not enough air for fuels to burn completely. We call this **incomplete combustion**.

 7 Why does incomplete combustion happen?

Look at the diagrams to see the different products of complete and incomplete combustion of methane.

With the air hole closed, water and carbon are formed.

Water and carbon dioxide are formed when the air hole is open.

With the air hole half-open, water and carbon monoxide are formed.

This is the reaction when the air hole is half-open:

methane + oxygen → carbon monoxide + hydrogen oxide + energy

$$2CH_4 + 3O_2 \rightarrow 2CO + 4H_2O + energy$$

When the air hole is closed even less oxygen is available from the air:

methane + oxygen → carbon + hydrogen oxide + energy

$$CH_4 + O_2 \rightarrow C + 2H_2O + energy$$

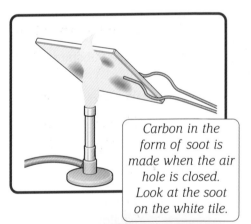

Carbon in the form of soot is made when the air hole is closed. Look at the soot on the white tile.

 8 As you slowly close the air hole of a Bunsen burner what gas is cut off from the flame?

9 Which gas provides the carbon that appears as soot in the flame?

 10 Describe how a 'safe' Bunsen burner flame in a school laboratory uses incomplete combustion to show that the Bunsen burner is lit.

The small dust-like particles of soot become very hot in the flame. They glow like thousands of miniature lamps, making the flame yellow and luminous. This is how candles, oil lamps and lanterns make light by burning a fuel.

Incomplete combustion can be dangerous

Gas fires and gas central heating boilers use methane as fuel. If there is plenty of air, carbon dioxide and water are formed. They escape out of a type of chimney called a flue.

Incomplete combustion happens when too little air reaches the flame. The flame contains carbon monoxide gas and is yellow with glowing carbon. Carbon monoxide is poisonous and has no smell.

You can sometimes see the water produced in combustion as steam.

Two students die – faulty gas fire blamed

11 How can you tell if a gas fire is not working properly?

12 Find out why you should not put damp washing on top of gas fires and central heating boilers, even if you think there is very little chance of the washing catching fire.

Incomplete combustion causes pollution

Vehicle fuels are hydrocarbons and are never completely burnt. Carbon dioxide, carbon monoxide, oxides of nitrogen made from burnt nitrogen, water and sometimes soot are formed. Most of these substances are harmful pollutants in our air.

13 Find out how the oxides of nitrogen are made by combustion in a hot car engine.

You can see the water as steam from a car's exhaust on a cold day. You cannot see the colourless pollutant carbon monoxide.

Matches, fireworks and explosives

Chemicals can be used in spectacular ways in very rapid combustion reactions. These uses of chemistry are called <u>pyrotechnics</u>.

Special chemicals containing their own oxygen are used in pyrotechnics.

Some chemicals contain the oxygen needed for combustion in their molecules. Examples are potassium nitrate (KNO_3), potassium chlorate ($KClO_3$) and potassium permanganate ($KMnO_4$). These compounds contain a lot of oxygen atoms.

14 How many oxygen atoms are there in one molecule of:

a potassium nitrate;

b potassium chlorate;

c potassium permanganate?

Compounds containing two elements and oxygen have names ending in '-ate'. Some of these compounds are called <u>oxidising agents</u>, because they are good at giving up oxygen to other chemicals. Adding oxygen like this is called **oxidation**.
The oxygen in the oxidising agents can rapidly react with other chemicals to cause explosions, even under water.

15 How are the three potassium compounds named to show that they contain oxygen?

Combustion using the oxygen in an oxidising agent makes a fast reaction called an explosion.

How matches work

Match heads contain a mixture of chemicals. They use the reaction between sulphur and phosphorus and an oxidising agent called potassium chlorate.

16 Write down the formula for potassium chlorate and the symbols for sulphur and phosphorus.

Friction when you strike a match makes the oxidising agent release oxygen. The sulphur and phosphorus burn in the oxygen, giving out a lot of heat.

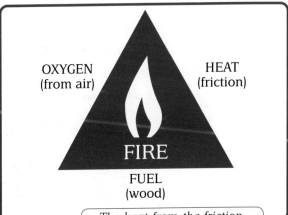

OXYGEN (from air)   HEAT (friction)

FIRE

FUEL (wood)

The heat from the friction, the wood in the match and oxygen in the air make a fire triangle, so the match burns.

17 What is the fuel in the burning match, as shown in the fire triangle?

18 What group of chemicals provides the heat in the triangle?

9H.2 Chemical reactions as energy resources

Chemicals make other useful forms of energy besides heat. For example, we use chemicals in **cells** and batteries to make electricity.

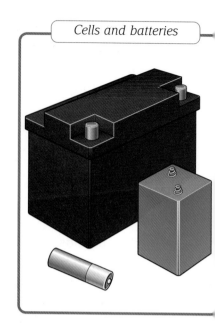

1 Why do we often use cells, instead of a mains supply, as a source of electricity?

There are many types of cells. The different types have special names such as nickel–cadmium, lead–acid or lithium cells. Many cells contain elements such as zinc, copper, lead, manganese, mercury or silver. These elements are metals. Metals are nearly always used in cells. Even gold has been used.

2 What sort of element is most often used to make a cell?

You can use a pair of different metals dipped into dilute sulphuric acid to make a cell. The pieces of metal that dip into the acid are called <u>electrodes</u>.

Different pairs of metals dipped in acid produce different voltages.

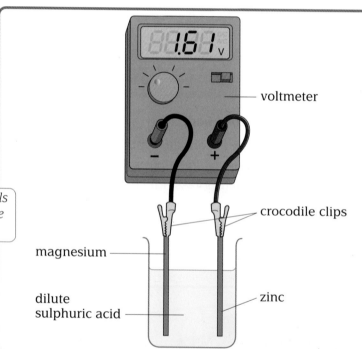

voltmeter

crocodile clips

magnesium

zinc

dilute sulphuric acid

The voltage produced depends on the difference in reactivity between the two metals.

Negative electrode	Positive electrode	Approximate reading on the voltmeter
magnesium	copper	2.71 V
magnesium	iron	1.93 V
magnesium	zinc	1.61 V

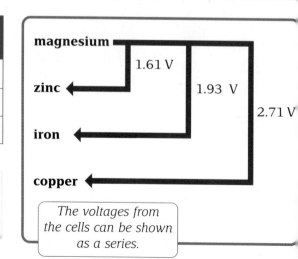

magnesium

1.61 V

zinc

1.93 V

iron

2.71 V

copper

The voltages from the cells can be shown as a series.

3 Which pair of metals would make the best cell?

4 Work out how many volts you get from a cell that uses zinc and copper electrodes.

Scientists put metals in very special and carefully controlled cells and measured the voltages produced. Look at their results.

K	3.26 V	Zn	1.11 V
Na	3.05 V	Fe	0.78 V
Mg	2.71 V	Pb	0.47 V
Al	2.00 V	Cu	0.00 V

This series is called the **electrochemical series**.

5 Which metal is the highest in the series and which metal is the lowest?

Reactivity of metals

In Unit 9F you saw how to construct and use a reactivity series of metals. You also saw how to compare pairs of metals by using <u>displacement reactions</u>. Displacement reactions happen when a reactive metal is placed in a solution of a salt of a less reactive metal. For example:

zinc + copper sulphate → zinc sulphate + copper

Zn + $CuSO_4$ → $ZnSO_4$ + Cu

6 Is zinc higher up or lower down the electrochemical series than copper?

7 Do you think magnesium will displace copper from copper sulphate solution? Explain your answer.

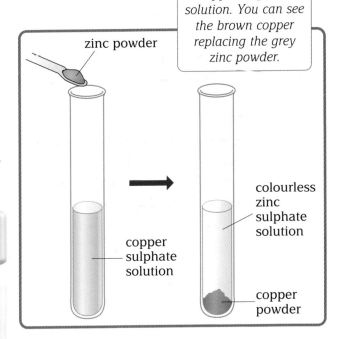

The reactive zinc displaces the less reactive copper from copper sulphate solution. You can see the brown copper replacing the grey zinc powder.

zinc powder

colourless zinc sulphate solution

copper sulphate solution

copper powder

Copper, silver and gold are unreactive metals, so people have them to make coins for thousands of years.

Silver is an unreactive metal and is even more unreactive than copper. Experiments with cells show that copper gives a voltage when paired with silver. Silver is so unreactive that it gives a negative reading on the voltmeter.

Cu	0.00 V
Ag	−0.46 V

Copper should displace silver from a solution of a silver salt.

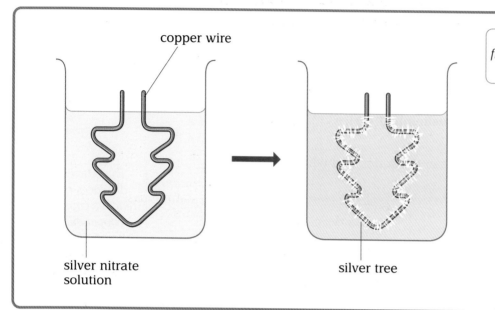

copper wire

silver nitrate
solution

silver tree

The copper displaces the silver
from the silver nitrate solution to
make a 'silver tree'.

The equation for the displacement of silver by copper is:

copper + silver nitrate → silver + copper nitrate

$$Cu + 2AgNO_3 \rightarrow 2Ag + Cu(NO_3)_2$$

8 Predict another reaction between a metal and silver
nitrate that might be a displacement reaction.

Heat and reactions

There are many chemical reactions that produce temperature
changes but do not involve combustion. For example, heat is
released when concentrated sulphuric acid is diluted and when
plaster of Paris sets.

Palm
HOT
Warmers
Wow it's WARM!

**Hand & Pocket
warmer**

Tear here >>>

Hand warmers use
heat from a chemical
reaction that does not
use combustion.

9 Why do you think that sulphuric acid is not used in
hand warmers?

9H.3 What new materials can chemical reactions make?

Chemists keep finding new ways to make useful molecules from basic resources such as minerals and plants.

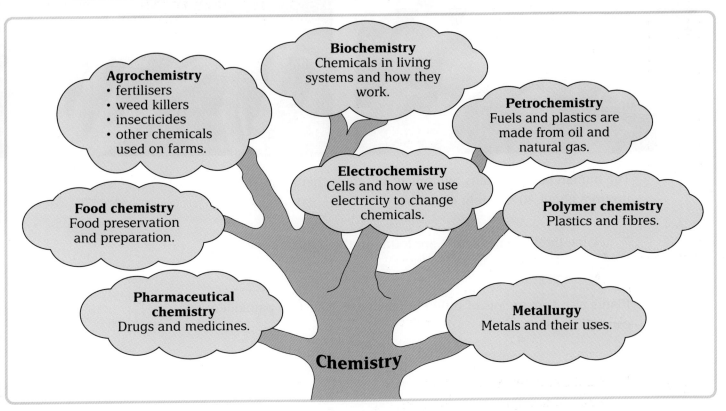

Agrochemistry
- fertilisers
- weed killers
- insecticides
- other chemicals used on farms.

Biochemistry
Chemicals in living systems and how they work.

Petrochemistry
Fuels and plastics are made from oil and natural gas.

Food chemistry
Food preservation and preparation.

Electrochemistry
Cells and how we use electricity to change chemicals.

Polymer chemistry
Plastics and fibres.

Pharmaceutical chemistry
Drugs and medicines.

Metallurgy
Metals and their uses.

Chemistry

1   Name <u>four</u> chemicals produced or used by your body.

2   List <u>three</u> fuels made by the petrochemical industry.

3   List <u>three</u> different artificial fabrics.

4   Find out which metals are used to make modern coins. Write your answer using chemical symbols.

5   Look at the different types of cells used in your house. Draw a diagram of <u>two</u> types and write down their cell voltage.

6   Look at the labels on food jars, tins and packages, and list the chemicals in <u>three</u> of them.

Living materials contain very large and complicated molecules, such as proteins and DNA.

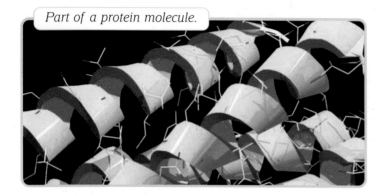

Part of a protein molecule.

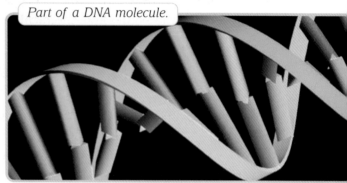

Part of a DNA molecule.

The human body contains millions of different chemicals, made up from about 40 different elements.

7 Name <u>three</u> elements that are found in the human body.

Plants also contain lots of different chemicals. Our first painkillers came from plants.

How we got Aspirin

Hippocrates was a Greek philosopher who lived about 2500 years ago. He studied and practised medicine. He used a medicine made from the bark and leaves of willow trees to cure headaches and other pains.

8 Write down <u>three</u> modern painkilling medicines.

In the 18th century, clergymen and doctors started to use willow as a painkiller again. They had discovered the idea in some ancient texts.

Hippocrates is known as the father of medicine.

9 Do you think that all natural plant medicines are safe?

People thought that willow trees contained a secret ingredient that could cure pain.

Scientists tried to find out which of the chemicals in the willow tree was the painkiller. In the 1820s they finally extracted and identified the painkilling chemical.

Unfortunately, salicin caused side effects such as stomach aches, it made some people feel sick and they got bad indigestion.

In 1899 a chemical company reacted salicin with other chemicals to change it. The new drug was tested on some patients in a **trial**. A trial is where animals and then volunteer patients are tested with a new drug before it goes on sale. The side effects were few and the drug was renamed 'aspirin'.

Salix is the Latin name for a willow tree, so the chemical was named 'salicin'.

10 Aspirin can be used as a medicine for many illnesses. Find out about <u>one</u> illness where aspirin can be used.

Making new molecules is called <u>synthesis</u>. New chemicals that do not occur in nature are often made by synthesis. So they are called <u>synthetic</u> materials. Scientists join atoms and molecules together in different ways with bonds.

9H.4 Atoms and molecules in new materials

Making and breaking bonds is chemistry

When chemical reactions happen, the bonds in the starting molecules are broken and new bonds are made in the molecules that you end up with. Energy is released or taken in to make these changes.

The models of molecules show what happens when barbecue charcoal burns. Bonds are broken. Then new bonds are made to make carbon dioxide.

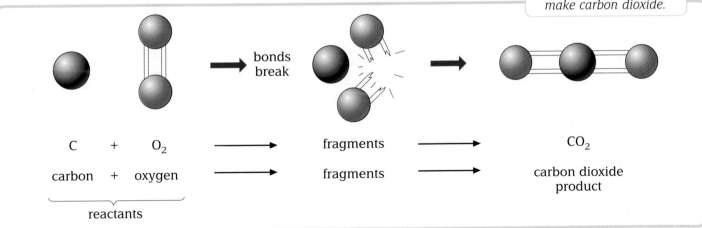

| C | + | O_2 | $\longrightarrow$ | fragments | $\longrightarrow$ | CO_2 |
| carbon | + | oxygen | $\longrightarrow$ | fragments | $\longrightarrow$ | carbon dioxide product |

reactants

1 Is energy released when charcoal burns?

The number of atoms is the same before and after the reaction. This means that the amount of material you have before the reaction starts and the amount you have when the reaction finishes are the same. No mass is lost. This rule is called the **law of conservation of mass**, and it works for all chemical reactions. In any reaction only the bonds are broken and made, not the atoms.

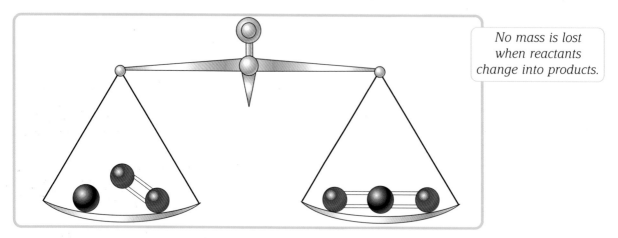

No mass is lost when reactants change into products.

When a candle burns, it looks like the law of conservation of mass is not being obeyed.

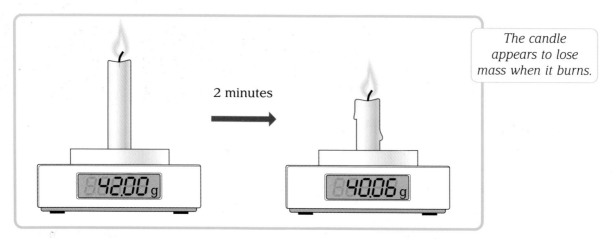

2 minutes

The candle appears to lose mass when it burns.

? 2 How much mass has the candle lost while burning?

When the candle burns, it uses up oxygen from the air and produces water vapour and carbon dioxide. These gases escape into the air and so the candle seems to lose mass.

? 3 Where does the lost mass of the candle go?

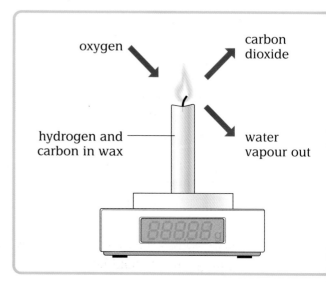

oxygen

carbon dioxide

hydrogen and carbon in wax

water vapour out

When all the oxygen, the escaping water vapour and the carbon dioxide are weighed, you can see that there is <u>no</u> change in mass. The law of conservation of mass <u>is</u> obeyed.

Burning a large mass of wood or a similar fuel seems to show a large loss of mass and leave just a little ash.

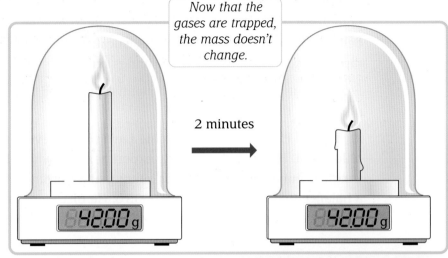

Now that the gases are trapped, the mass doesn't change.

2 minutes

4 Where does the mass of the burning wood go?

A theory about burning

In the late 1600s, two German chemists, called Johann Becher and Georg Stahl, made a new theory about burning. They thought metals, minerals and substances that could burn contained a substance called '**phlogiston**'. Phlogiston was given out during combustion in the form of fire, flames and light.

Scientists thought that:

- phlogiston was taken up by the air;

- there was a limit to the amount of phlogiston the air could take up;

- if you burned a candle in a closed vessel, the flame soon went out because the air inside had taken up all the phlogiston it could hold.

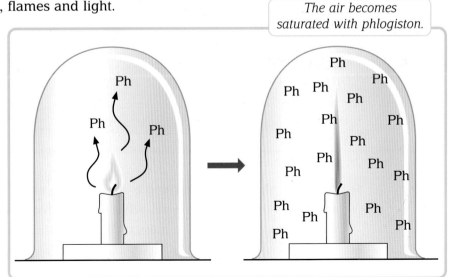

The air becomes saturated with phlogiston.

Normal air was called 'dephlogisticated' because it contained no phlogiston. When Joseph Priestley discovered <u>oxygen</u>, he believed it to be the purest 'dephlogisticated' air, which would rapidly take up phlogiston when things burned.

From about 1680 to 1800 most scientists accepted the phlogiston theory.

At first the French scientist Antoine Lavoisier believed in phlogiston. He carried out many experiments in which he weighed things before and after heating and burning. He used a balance that could weigh to 0.0005 g. He discovered that substances <u>gained</u> mass from the air when they burned.

5 If the phlogiston theory is true, what should happen to the mass when something burns?

From his experiments, Lavoisier discovered the law of conservation of mass as well as the role of oxygen in combustion. On the 5th September 1775, Lavoisier presented his ideas to the French Academy of Science. This is a translation of parts of the paper he published in 1777:

Antoine Lavoisier lived during the time of the French Revolution. It was a time when many old ideas and theories were challenged.

> *I venture to propose to the Academy today a new theory of combustion. Materials may not burn except in a very few kinds of air, or rather, combustion may take place in only a single variety of air: that which ... has been named dephlogisticated air and which I name here pure air. In all combustion, pure air in which the combustion takes place is destroyed or decomposed and the burning body increases in weight exactly in proportion to the quantity of air destroyed or decomposed.*

This paper destroyed the theory of phlogiston. Soon no one believed in phlogiston. All scientists now agreed that oxygen was used in combustion.

6 Lavoisier showed that burning a substance in air decreases the mass of the air. What did the phlogiston theory say happens to the mass of the air during burning?

7 From our knowledge today, which gases do you think make up 'dephlogisticated' air?

You should now understand the key words and key ideas shown below.

There is never a loss or gain of mass in chemical reactions. This rule is called the **law of conservation of mass**.

The **electrochemical series** can be used to predict displacement reactions.

Cells made of pairs of metals in acid make different voltages and can be put in a list called the electrochemical series.

When new materials are made in a chemical reaction, the bonds in the molecules are broken and new bonds are made.

Cells and batteries use metals and other chemicals to make useful electricity.

Useful chemistry

Chemistry is used to make useful energy, to keep us well fed and healthy, and to make useful new materials.

Some chemical reactions give out heat energy without flames or combustion, and are used as hand warmers.

Trials are the tests that scientists carry out before a new product goes on sale.

North Sea gas is an important fuel and contains methane. Methane is a **hydrocarbon**, which means it contains hydrogen and carbon only.

Combustion involves adding oxygen from the air to chemicals to make energy and new substances called oxides.

Complete combustion happens when methane burns completely in air, to make carbon dioxide and hydrogen oxide (water).

Oxidation occurs when oxygen is added to other chemicals.

Incomplete combustion of methane happens when there is not enough oxygen available.

The '**phlogiston**' theory was popular for two centuries until oxygen and oxides were discovered. Theories about combustion had to change.

Scientific investigations

Throughout Key Stage 3 you will look at investigations carried out by scientists, past and present, and carry out your own investigations. This chapter will remind you of the skills you learnt at Key Stage 2 and will help you to practise and improve them. It will also introduce new skills.

Planning investigations

Finding suitable questions for investigations

When you do an investigation, you have a question to answer. Then you plan an investigation that you hope will give you the answer. But you can't answer all questions by doing a scientific investigation.

1   Look at parts **a** to **c**. Can you answer them by doing a scientific investigation? Explain your answers.

   a Is there a link between the height of a cat and the length of its whiskers?

   b Where is the rainiest place on Earth? (You can't visit everywhere on Earth, but lots of scientists have collected data about rainfall in lots of places.)

   c Are waterfalls beautiful? (Think about whether people agree on what is beautiful!)

Now think about the question of why elephants throw water over themselves. You can't answer it directly, but you can do an investigation using a model.

First, you need to think of <u>ideas</u> that might explain why elephants throw water over themselves. We call these ideas **hypotheses**.

Elephants often spray water over themselves like this.

KEY WORDS
hypotheses
prediction
sample size
sampling
random
surveys
secondary data
relevant
reliable
accurate
validity of results
preliminary tests
variable
vary
control
range
scale
precision
hazards
risk
risk assessment
mean
bar chart
line graph
data collection
presenting results
conclusion
evidence
evaluation
anomalous results
opinions
biased

The idea that elephants do this to cool themselves is one that you can test. You probably haven't got an elephant, so you have to use a model! A plastic bottle full of hot water makes a suitable model. You can use a thermometer or a temperature probe and a datalogger to show any temperature changes.

The elephants are:
* just having a wash;
* trying to cool themselves;
* getting rid of parasites;
* chasing away flies;
* just playing.

2 Draw your idea of what the model elephant apparatus looks like.

3 Remember that you are trying to find out if water makes the elephants cooler.

    a Describe how to model throwing the water over the elephant.

    b What measurements will you need to write down?

Next, you need to say what you think your results will be. This is called making a **prediction**. You need to use the science that you know to give reasons for your prediction. Kirsty has made a prediction:

I think that when we pour cold water over the plastic bottle, the temperature of the water inside will fall.

4 Do you think that Kirsty's prediction is correct? Explain your answer as fully as you can. Remember that an explanation using scientific ideas will get you the best marks.

Choosing the best strategy for an investigation

Often there are several possible ways of doing an investigation. However, one method may be better than the others. For example, one way may be easier, safer or produce more useful data than all the other methods.

You are likely to have done investigations involving fair testing in which you learnt about the importance of controlling variables. However, some variables are easier to control than others. Physical factors such as light and temperature are fairly easy to control.

Living things are a particular problem because they themselves vary. So when you investigate living things, you use 10 or 20 or more, not just one. We call this using a sample. You have to think about a suitable **sample size**. In *Spectrum Biology* Unit 8D you learn how to estimate the numbers of different living things by **sampling** using quadrats.

*By taking a sample of 20 **random** quadrats, these pupils are allowing for the fact that conditions are not the same in all parts of the beach.*

5 Explain why the sample needs to be random.

You can also use sampling to do **surveys** of data about people, including people's opinions. These often involve questionnaires.

Information collected by other people is useful in some investigations. We call the information **secondary data**. Examples are the data in leaflets produced by companies, consumer reports, libraries and the Internet. You need to be careful as some of this information may be biased.

You can find out information from secondary sources such as this.

6 List some secondary sources of information about factors affecting the pH of soil.

Collecting appropriate data

To answer your question, the data that you collect must be relevant, reliable and accurate. So you need to:

- choose a suitable design of your investigation to ensure that your evidence is **relevant**. That is why scientists often do trial runs. Relevant evidence is evidence that will help you to answer your question;

- record sufficient observations or readings to ensure that your evidence is **reliable**;

- choose suitable measuring instruments and take accurate and precise readings to ensure that your evidence is **accurate**.

The **validity of results** depends on the accuracy and precision of the <u>measuring instruments</u> that you choose and <u>how well you use them</u>.

Using preliminary work such as trial runs

Scientists often do trial runs of experiments to find out whether their approach will work or not.

Mrs Tasker asked her class to find out which of three varieties of apples gave the most juice by finding out how much of each apple is water. She set her class some preliminary work using books to research a method. No one found that actual experiment, but Bryan found one about the amount of water in soil. Using the same idea, he suggested an experiment:

- Find the mass of an apple.
- Heat it to get rid of all the water.
- Find its mass again. The loss in mass will be equal to the mass of water that was in the apple.

Anna found out that you needed to repeat this several times until two masses were the same. It is called heating to constant mass and you do it so you can be sure that all the water has gone. Lee thought that chopping the apple might make drying faster.
Mrs Tasker was pleased with the ideas so far – but she pointed out that they hadn't described how to heat the apple.

She suggested that they needed to do some **preliminary tests**. They needed to try out their ideas to find out which one worked best.

7 What <u>two</u> kinds of preliminary work did the class do before they planned their investigation?

	Heat over Bunsen flame		Dry on an open shelf at 20°C		Heat in an oven at 100°C		Heat in an oven at 300°C	
Size of apple pieces	cut into 1/8ths	chopped up small	cut into 1/8ths	chopped up small	cut into 1/8ths	chopped up small	cut into 1/8ths	chopped up small
Mass at start (g)	140.8	136.4	142.3	143.5	138.6	136.7	133.6	139.1
Mass after 40 mins (g)	12.7	10.1	137.6	135.2	103.5	100.8	10.9	10.1
Mass after 1 day (g)	not done	not done	69.1	67.7	17.3	16.2	9.4	8.4
Mass after 7 days (g)	not done	not done	28.5	28.9	17.3	16.2	not done	not done
Loss in mass (g)	128.1	126.3	113.8	114.6	121.3	120.5	124.2	130.7
% loss in mass	91	92.5	80	80	87.5	88	93	94
Observations	black (burnt)	black (burnt)	brown and mouldy	brown and mouldy	brown	brown	black (burnt)	black (burnt)

Results of preliminary tests.

8 The pupils rejected heating over a Bunsen and in an oven at 300°C because the apple lost more than just water.

  a What evidence is there that more than just water was lost?

  b Suggest what else was lost.

9 Suggest <u>two</u> problems of drying the apple at 20°C.

10 These tests didn't show whether chopping up the apple made a difference to the time taken to dry the apple. What extra tests can the class do to find out the answer?

11 In the final plan for their investigation, why did the pupils:

  a chop up the apples;

  b find the mass of the apples on a digital balance;

  c heat in an oven at 100°C;

  d heat to constant mass?

12 Write a list of other ideas that the pupils probably used to make their investigation safe and their results valid.

Controlling variables

In an experiment, lots of things affect the results.
We call these **variables**.

To find out the effect of temperature on dissolving salt, you **vary**
the temperature but keep the other things the same. We say that
you **control** them. This is to make your test fair.

It makes it easier to spot a pattern in your results if you use a
wide **range** for your variable. For example, your results may be
too similar to be sure of the pattern if you use only a small range
of temperatures.

13 Write down <u>two</u> things that you need to control or keep
the same when you investigate the effect of temperature
on dissolving.

Selecting equipment

Some choices of equipment are easy but you need to be particularly
careful when you choose measuring equipment. Instruments for
measuring have a **scale** on them. You need to choose the
instrument with a suitable scale for your particular investigation.

For example, measuring the mass of a small strip of magnesium
on kitchen scales would not give you a useful reading. A chemical
balance would be much more useful. The choice affects the
precision of your results.

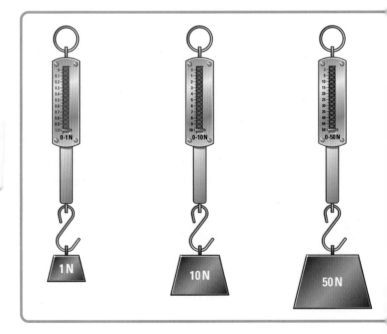

salt solution

*The temperature of the water,
the size of the crystals and the
amount of stirring all affect
the time it takes for the salt to
dissolve. These are all variables*

Sean is investigating the force needed
to pick up objects in the lab.
He estimates that the weight of
these objects varies from 5N to 45N.

14 Choose the best forcemeter for
Sean's investigation.
Explain your choice.

Safety

Sometimes you need to use apparatus or chemicals that can be harmful. We call these things **hazards**. You can use them only if you make sure that you and other people are safe. You can look up some hazards in books and others on Hazcards, or you can ask your teacher for help.

Next you need to ask yourself how high a **risk** there is of the hazard causing harm. We call this a **risk assessment**. You do this to decide whether your investigation is safe enough to do. Sometimes the risk assessment helps you to see how to make your investigation safe, for example by wearing eye protection.

15 Where can you find out about possible hazards?

16 What must you do if you are not sure that your investigation is safe enough?

Obtaining and presenting evidence

Before you start an investigation, you need to know exactly:
- what you are going to do;
- what results you are going to record;
- how you are going to record your results, for example in a table on paper or using a datalogger.

Collecting appropriate data

You don't always get the same results from the same experiment. To find out what is really happening, you have to:
- do your experiment several times;
- work out the average result. You find the average by adding together your results and dividing by the number of results. This is sometimes called the **mean**.

Often you can use a range of sources of information and data in an investigation. The more data you have, the easier it is to be confident about your conclusion. A whole class set of results produces even more accurate and reliable data.

17 Why is it more accurate to have several sets of data?

Hazardous chemicals have warning labels. You need to be able to recognise them.

CORROSIVE

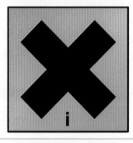

This is the sign for an irritant.

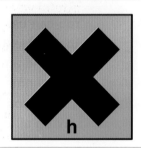

This is the sign for a harmful substance.

Presenting results as bar charts or graphs

Often you need to show results in ways that will help you to see any trends and patterns. For example, as a **bar chart** or a **line graph**.

You can use a bar chart to compare one piece of information with another. A line graph shows how a variable changes. You need to choose the best kind of chart or graph for your data as well as a suitable scale for each axis.

Usually when you are plotting a bar chart or a line graph, the variable that you changed goes along the bottom (x-axis) and the one you measured goes up the side (y-axis).

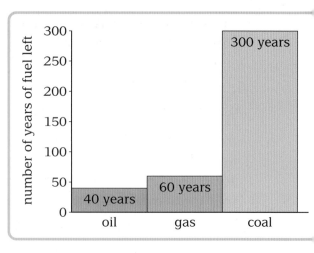

Using computers to collect data and present results

The Internet is a source of information for some investigations. You can also use a computer for **data collection** and **presenting results**.

You can use dataloggers with sensors to record different sorts of environmental changes, for example temperature, amount of light and amount of dissolved oxygen. You can also use them to log the times of readings. So data can be collected over 24 hours without you having to remember to take readings or having to stay up all night.

You can plot the results of experiments, whether collected by hand or with a datalogger, using a spreadsheet program. Careful plotting can make results easier to read. When you get used to using a spreadsheet for plotting graphs, it will also save you time.

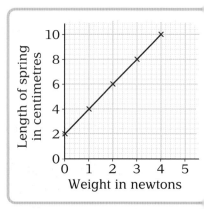

 18 What are the advantages in using a datalogger?

Considering evidence

Identifying trends

Tables, charts and graphs allow you to identify any trends and patterns in your data and to pick out results that do not fit the pattern.

Coming to conclusions

The **conclusion** is where you say what you have found out, so it is an important part of your investigation. You need to describe any trends or patterns and the evidence that supports your conclusion. You should also try to use scientific ideas to explain why you got the results that you did.

Evaluating evidence

Measurement and observation are part of the process of collecting **evidence** to support an explanation or theory. The last part of any investigation is to carry out an **evaluation**. You need to look at the evidence and decide:

- whether there is enough evidence to support a conclusion;
- how you could improve your investigation to increase the strength of your evidence;
- whether or not things presented as evidence are <u>actually evidence</u>.

For example, perhaps you could have:

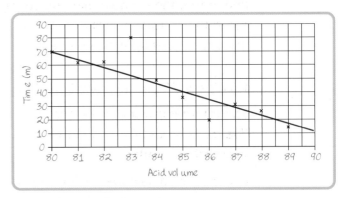

- taken readings more accurately;
- taken more readings;
- repeated readings.

You also need to try to spot any results that do not fit the general pattern. These are called **anomalous results**.

Look at the graph showing a line of best fit.

19 Some points on the graph do not lie near the line of best fit. What can you do to improve this set of readings?

Sometimes people give their **opinions**. They may have no evidence for their ideas. Their opinions may be **biased**. They are conclusions that, if correct, would benefit them in some way.

In experimental investigations, you are probably used to evaluating the number and accuracy of readings and know how to deal with readings that don't fit the pattern. You assume that the work of other people who contributed results is accurate and honest. In some other investigations, for example life-style surveys, people don't always tell the truth.

20 a Sometimes smokers deny that they smoke. Suggest reasons.

  b Write down three other life-style or health issues where people sometimes hide the truth.

So, sometimes evidence is gathered inaccurately and sometimes it is incomplete. When your evidence is incomplete, you may find that your explanation turns out to be wrong. This shows just how careful you have to be when you consider and evaluate evidence.

Glossary/Index

Words in *italics* are themselves defined in the glossary.

A

abrasion   wear caused by one *substance* rubbing against another   84, 88

absorb, absorption   when an object or *substance* takes in another object or substance. When living *cells* or *blood* take in *dissolved nutrients* or *oxygen*   72

accurate, accuracy   correct, *precise* and without any mistakes; accurate *evidence* is gathered using accurate measuring instruments with *precision*   108–109, 123, 134, 158, 161, 163

acid, acidic   a *solution* that *reacts* with many *metals* to produce a *salt* and *hydrogen*, and with *alkalis* to produce a salt and water   1–14, 17–18, 25, 68, 72, 79, 91, 102–106, 108, 110, 114, 123, 125–132, 134–136, 140, 146, 148, 155

acid rain   rain that is more *acidic* than rain normally is because it has *sulphur dioxide* or *nitrogen oxides* dissolved in it   79, 128–132, 134–136, 140

air   a *mixture* of *gases*, mainly *nitrogen* and *oxygen*   18, 20–23, 29–30, 34–36, 56, 65–66, 71–74, 76, 79, 131–132, 134–144, 152–154

air quality   how clean or polluted the *air* is   134–136, 140

alkali, alkaline   chemicals that *neutralise acids* to produce *salts*   3–14, 68, 99, 101, 106–108, 110, 112, 125

alkali metals   soft, *reactive* metals in Group 1 of the *Periodic Table*; they *react* with water to produce *hydrogen* and an *alkaline solution*   112, 125

alloy   a *mixture* of metals   99–100

Anning, Mary   (1799–1847)   87

anomalous results   results that do not fit the general pattern   163

argon   an *inert* or *noble gas* that makes up about 1% of the *air*   71–72, 74, 76

atmosphere   the layer of *air* above the Earth's surface   115, 125, 131, 138, 140

atom   the smallest *particle* of an *element*   53, 56–57, 59, 62–66, 69, 76, 104, 145, 152

attracted, attraction   two objects pulling towards each other   32–33, 36, 38, 47, 52, 111

B

bar chart   a way of *presenting results*   162

basalt   an *igneous rock* with small grains because it formed from a *magma* that cooled quickly   80, 94–95, 98

battery   made from two or more electrical *cells* joined together   146, 155

Becher, Johann   (1635–1682)   153

biased, bias   in the case of an *opinion*, based on someone's feelings rather than all the facts   136, 158, 163

blood   a *liquid* in animal circulatory systems   72

boiling point   the *temperature* at which a *liquid* changes into a *gas*   33, 73–76

bonds   links between *atoms* in *molecules*   151–152, 155

breathe, breathing   taking *air* in and out of the *lungs*   65, 71–72, 134

bronchitis   an infection of the air tubes in the *lungs*   135

Brown, Robert   (1773–1858)   29–31

Brownian motion   *random* movement of *particles*   29–31, 38

burn, burning when *substances react* with *oxygen* and release *energy*; also called *combustion* 18–24, 60, 68, 73, 132, 139, 141–145, 151–155

C

calcium a *metal element*; a *mineral nutrient* that living things need 58, 70, 80

car exhaust emissions waste *gases* from car exhausts 132–136

carbon a *non-metallic element* 22, 58, 101, 121, 125, 139–144, 151–152, 155

carbon dioxide a *gas* in the *air* produced by living things in *respiration*, in *combustion* or *burning* and when an *acid reacts* with a *carbonate* 11–12, 17, 19, 21, 23–24, 57, 59, 62–63, 66, 68, 71, 73, 76, 79, 91, 104, 131–133, 138–144, 151–153, 155

carbon monoxide a poisonous *gas* 133–134, 143–144

carbonate a *compound* that *reacts* with *acids* to produce *carbon dioxide*; *limestone* is *calcium carbonate* 17, 24, 62, 66, 68, 79, 86, 91, 104, 106, 126, 129

catalytic converter in a car exhaust system, it changes nitrogen monoxide and *carbon monoxide* pollutants to *nitrogen* and *carbon dioxide* 133–134, 140

cell (in biology) building block of plants and animals

cell (in physics) uses a *chemical reaction* to push an *electric current* around an *electric circuit* 146–147, 149, 154

Celsius a *temperature scale* with the *melting point* of ice written as 0 °C and the *boiling point* of water as 100 °C

chemical change, reaction a *reaction* between chemicals; it produces a new *substance* 15–17, 24, 60, 63–64, 67–68, 89, 93, 104–105, 107, 116, 141, 148, 151

chemical equation a *word equation* or *symbol equation* that shows what happens in a *chemical reaction* 63–64

chemical weathering when *chemical reactions* cause the *weathering* or breakdown of rocks 79–80, 88

chromatogram the separated *substances* that are the result of *chromatography* 47–49, 52

chromatography a way of separating a *mixture* of *dissolved solids* 47–49, 52

classify sort things into groups 97

climate change changes in climate patterns such as those caused by *global warming* 139

combustion when *substances react* with *oxygen* and release *energy*; another word for *burning* 18, 24, 68, 141–143, 145, 148, 153–155

complete combustion when a substance *burns* completely, becoming totally *oxidised* 142, 155

components *devices* used in *electric circuits*

compound a *substance* made from the *atoms* of two or more different *elements* joined together 61–69, 71, 75–76, 104, 116, 118–120, 141–142, 145

compress to squeeze into a smaller space 33

concentration the strength of a *solution* or the amount of a *substance* in a *mixture* 86, 135

conclusion what you have found out 135–136, 161–163

condense, condensation when a *gas* cools and changes into a *liquid* 33, 45–46, 52, 73

condenser a piece of equipment used in *distillation* 46, 52

conduction, conduct (i) in heat conduction, *energy* passes along a *solid* as its *particles* heat up and *vibrate* faster. A conductor of *heat energy* will let heat energy pass through it; (ii) in electrical conduction, an *electric current* flows though a *substance* 37–38, 99–101

conservation of mass a scientific law stating that no loss of *mass* happens in a *chemical reaction* 43, 152–155

contract become smaller; *solids*, *liquids* and *gases* do this when they cool 60, 82

control the part of an experiment that is needed to make a test fair, where certain *variables* are controlled or kept the same while one variable is varied; it is needed so that we can be sure of the cause of a change or a difference 157, 160

corrosion the disappearance or change of *substances* such as *metals* when they *react* with chemicals such as *acids* or with water and *oxygen* 16, 24, 111, 130, 140

corrosive *substances* such as *acids* and *alkalis* that *dissolve* or eat away other *materials* 2, 14, 161

crystal, crystalline a *substance* that forms from a *melted* or a *dissolved solid* in a definite shape 29, 32, 41–42, 54, 57, 61, 67, 79, 85–86, 94–95, 102, 104–105, 160

crystallisation when *crystals* form from a *melted* or a *dissolved solid* 42

D

Dalton, John (1766–1844) 56

data information, for example facts or numbers 51, 134–135, 137, 157–158, 161–162

data collection gathering *data* by any method 162

Davy, Humphry (1778–1829) 121

Democritus (about 460–370 BC) 27–29, 31, 56

density the *mass* per unit volume of a *substance* 99–100

deposit, deposition when *eroded* rock fragments settle 83, 85–86, 88, 97

Desaulx 30–31

device something that changes *energy* from one form into another 109

diatomic made up of two *atoms*; O_2 is an example 63

diffusion, diffuse the spreading out of a *gas* or a *dissolved substance* because its *particles* are moving at *random* 34, 38

digest, digestion the breakdown of large, *insoluble molecules* into small *soluble* ones which can be *absorbed* 60

dilute a dilute *solution* is a weak solution containing very little *dissolved solute*; to dilute a solution, you add more *solvent* 2, 14, 104, 108–109, 129–130, 148

displacement reaction, displace when a more *reactive* element pushes a less reactive *element* out of one of its *compounds* 116, 117, 125, 147–148, 155

dissolve, dissolved when the *particles* of a *substance* completely mix with the particles of a *liquid* to make a clear *solution* 3, 10, 13, 39–44, 47–52, 70–71, 79–80, 85–86, 88, 131–132, 160, 162

distillation *boiling* or *evaporating* a *liquid* and then *condensing* it to get a *pure* liquid 45–46, 52, 74

drug a *substance* that can change the way that your body works; to treat a *disease* 149–151

E

Einstein, Albert (1879–1955) 30–31

electric circuit *components* connected together to allow an *electric current* to flow

electric current flows around a complete *electric circuit* 121

electrical energy the *energy* in wires when *electric current* flows

electrochemical series a list of *metals* in order of the *voltages* produced when they are used in *cells* 147, 155

electrodes these are connected to a power supply and put into a *melted* or *dissolved substance* so that *electrolysis* can happen 63, 121, 146

electrolysis the process of splitting up a *melted* or *dissolved compound* by passing an *electric current* through it 63, 121, 125

element a *substance* that can't be split into anything simpler by *chemical reactions* 19, 53–55, 57–62, 64–67, 69, 75–76, 101–102, 105, 110, 112, 116, 118–119, 141, 145–146, 150

emissions pollutant *gases* given out from car exhausts, power stations etc. 133–134, 136, 140

energy energy is needed to make things happen 72, 83–84, 141, 143, 151, 155

environment the surroundings or conditions in which plants and animals live 87, 111

erosion, eroded wearing away of rocks involving the movement of the rock fragments away from where they formed 83, 88, 97–98, 126, 140

erupt, eruption when *lava, volcanic ash* and *gases* come out onto the surface of the Earth 95–96, 98

evaluation considering whether there is enough *evidence* to support a *conclusion* and whether an investigation can be improved 163

evaporate, evaporation when a *liquid* changes into a *gas* 41–43, 45–46, 52, 71, 86, 88, 94, 102, 104–105, 107

evidence *observations* and measurements on which *theories* are based 25–27, 29, 31, 38, 56, 96, 158–159, 161–163

Exner, F.M. 30–31

expand, expansion when a *substance* gets bigger because its *particles* speed up and move further apart 36–38, 60, 74, 81–82, 88, 129

explosion, explosive sudden rapid *burning* 20, 24

extract a *substance* taken from or made from another substance; examples are the juices taken from plants that we use as *indicators* 5–6, 14, 42, 119–122, 151

F

fair test a test in which one *variable* is varied and other variables are *controlled* or kept the same 123

fertilisers you add these to soil to provide the *minerals* that plants need to grow 149

filter, filtration separating a *liquid* from undissolved *solids* by passing it through tiny holes, usually in paper 41, 44, 52, 102, 104–105

fire triangle a diagram showing the three things, *fuel*, heat and *oxygen*, needed to make a fire 20, 22, 24, 145

force a push or a pull 82–83, 160

formula uses *symbols* to show how many *atoms* of *elements* are joined together to form a *molecule* of an element or a *compound* 62–64, 66, 76, 145

fossil remains of plants and animals from long ago 86–88, 90, 98

fossil fuels *fuels* formed in the Earth's crust from the remains of living things; for example coal 21, 24, 132, 139

fractional distillation the separation of a *mixture* of *liquids* by *distillation* 74, 76

freezing, freeze when a *liquid* cools and becomes *solid* 33, 60, 75, 81, 88, 129

freezing point the *temperature* at which a *liquid* becomes a *solid* 94

friction a *force* when two surfaces rub past each other; it acts in the opposite direction to the direction in which something is moving 145

monitoring   testing on a regular basis to detect changes in a system   134–135, 140

N

Napoleon III   (1808–1873)   121

neutral   when a *solution* is neither *acidic* nor *alkaline*; it has a *pH* of 7   7, 9, 14, 108–109

neutralise, neutralisation   when an *acid reacts* with an *alkali* to make a *neutral solution* of a *salt* in water   9–14, 68, 106–109

nitrate   *salts* produced from nitric acid; important plant *nutrient* in *fertilisers*   103–104, 106, 148

nitrogen   a *gas* that makes up about four fifths of the *air*   58–59, 63, 71–72, 74, 76

nitrogen oxides   *compounds* of *nitrogen* and *oxygen* that help to cause *acid rain*   132–134

noble gases   another word for *inert gases*; a group of unreactive gases   72, 76

non-metal   *elements* that are not *metals*; they usually have the opposite *properties* to metals   18–19, 53, 58, 100–101, 110

non-porous   describes the *texture* of a rock without *pores*   78–79, 88, 90

nutrients   the food *materials* that *cells* use   126

O

observations   records of changes, similarities, differences and other features   25, 32, 125, 158, 163

obsidian   an *igneous rock* that cools so quickly that it is glassy, not *crystalline*; also called volcanic glass   95, 98

opinion   what someone thinks – but not supported by conclusive *evidence*   158, 163

ore   a rock from which a *metal* or other *element* is *extracted*   105, 110, 119, 122, 125

organ   structure in a plant or animal made of several different *tissues*

oxidation   *oxygen* joining with other *elements* to make *compounds* called *oxides*; examples are *burning*, *rusting* and *respiration*   68, 145, 155

oxides   *compounds* of *oxygen* and another *element*   18–19, 21, 24, 99, 101, 105–106, 115, 118, 121, 125, 141–142, 144–145, 155

oxygen   a *gas* that makes up about one fifth of the *air*   18–21, 23–24, 54, 56, 58–59, 61–63, 65–66, 68, 71–72, 74, 76, 111–112, 115, 119–121, 141–145, 151–155, 162

P

particle   a very small piece of *matter* that everything is made of   22, 27–38, 44, 47, 52, 56–57, 64, 66–67, 69, 76, 82, 84

particle diagram, model   a way of picturing *matter* as made up of moving *particles*; also called the *kinetic theory*   31–38, 66–67, 69

Periodic Table   a table of the *elements* arranged in order so that similar elements are in the same column or group   58, 64

pH   a scale 0–14 that tells you how *acidic* or *alkaline* a solution is   7–14, 101, 108–109, 127, 128, 130, 136, 140, 158

phlogiston   the phlogiston *theory* was an idea between 1680 and 1800 to explain *burning*; *materials* that could burn were thought to contain a *substance* called phlogiston   153–155

photosynthesis   a process in which plants use light energy, water and *carbon dioxide* to make glucose   138

pollen   contains the male sex cell of a flowering plant   29–31

pores   the spaces between grains in *porous* rocks   78, 81, 90, 92

porous describes the *texture* of a rock with *pores* 78, 88, 90

precision, precise *accuracy* of measurements and measuring instruments 108, 158, 160

predict, prediction to say what you think will happen 113, 115, 124–125, 139, 148, 157

preliminary tests tests, *trial* runs and information searches carried out to find out the best approach to an investigation 159

presenting results showing results in a way that makes them easy to read and understand 162

pressure how much pushing *force* there is on an area 35, 38, 74, 89, 93, 95, 97–98

Priestley, Joseph (1733–1804) 154

product a new *substance* made in a *chemical reaction* 16, 20, 24, 63, 67–68, 80, 108, 116, 143, 152

progressive depletion gradual decrease in the number and variety; often of living things 131

properties what a *material* is like, for example whether it *burns* or *conducts* electricity 3, 29, 33, 99–102, 110–111

pumice an *igneous rock*; a *lava* with lots of *gas* bubbles 95, 98

pure contains one *material* only 40, 45–46, 52, 54, 65, 69, 75–76, 116–117, 128

Q

quadrat an object, often a square frame, used for *sampling* living things 157

R

radiation (of heat) a method of heat transfer, where the *heat energy* is given out as infra-red waves 138

random by chance; random movement is in a direction that cannot be *predicted* 30–31, 38, 157

range the values between the lowest and the highest value fall within the range 75, 160

react, reaction what happens when chemicals join or separate 9–12, 14, 67–68, 72, 76, 79–80, 91, 102–105, 107–108, 110–116, 118, 121, 125, 130, 133, 145–146, 152, 155

reactant a *substance* that you start off with in a *chemical reaction* 16, 20, 24, 63, 67, 105, 151

reactive *reacts* easily 67–68, 111–118, 121, 124–125

reactivity how likely a *substance* is to *react* 113–114, 116, 118, 123, 125, 146–147

reactivity series a list of *elements* in order of how *reactive* they are 113–117, 124–125

recycle use *materials* over and over again 77, 97

relevant suitable for, or appropriate to, something; relevant *evidence* helps to answer a particular question 158

reliable when something can be trusted; reliable *evidence* is based on sufficient and *accurate data* 134, 158, 161

renewables *energy* sources that are constantly being replaced so will not run out 132

respiration the breakdown of food to release *energy* in living *cells* 68, 138

risk the chance of a *hazard* causing harm 2, 14, 161

risk assessment considering how high a *risk* there is of a *hazard* causing harm 161

rust, rusting the *corrosion* of *iron* in the presence of water and *oxygen* to form iron *oxide*, or rust 115, 130

S

salt a *compound* produced when an *acid reacts* with a *metal* or an *alkali*; the everyday name for common salt or *sodium chloride* 9–10, 14, 39–45, 49, 61–62, 67, 75, 102–107, 110–111, 114, 116–117, 123, 125, 160

sample, sampling take a small part to get an idea of the whole 157–158

sample size the number of things in a *sample* 157

sandstone a s*edimentary rock* made from sand 78–79, 85, 87–88, 92, 94, 98, 129

saturated solution a *solution* in which no more *solid* will *dissolve* 49, 51–52

scale a series of numbers used to measure or compare things 160

secondary data information that has been collected by other people 158

sediment rock fragments that settle on the bed of a river, lake or sea 83–86, 88–89, 97–98

sedimentary rocks rocks formed when *sediments* are compacted and cemented; *sandstone* and *limestone* are examples 79, 85–86, 88–91, 97–98

Smith, William (1769–1839) 87

sodium chloride common *salt*; a *compound* of sodium and chlorine 10, 42, 49–52, 57, 61–62, 67–68, 70, 106–107

sodium hydroxide a *compound* that *dissolves* in water to make an *alkali* 3–6, 8, 10–11, 14, 42, 107, 112

solid a *substance* that stays a definite shape 15, 22, 28–29, 32–33, 36–39, 41, 49–51, 56, 58, 70, 73–75, 79–80, 82, 85–86, 88, 93, 95

solidify change from a *liquid* into a *solid* that happens as a result of cooling 73, 88, 94–97

solubility a measure of how *soluble* a *substance* is 49–52

soluble able to *dissolve* 40–41, 47–50, 52, 80, 11

solute how we describe a *substance* that is *dissolved* in a *liquid* 40, 43–47, 50–52, 160

solution a *mixture* formed when a *solute dissolves* in a *solvent* 9–10, 39–47, 49, 52, 94, 101, 104, 108–109, 112, 116, 131, 147, 160

solvent a *liquid* in which other *substances* will *dissolve* 40, 43–44, 46–48, 50–52, 160

Stahl, George (1660–1734) 153

states of matter *solids*, *liquids* and *gases* are the three states of matter 28–29, 38

substances types of *matter* 3–5, 11, 15, 18–28, 30–32, 34, 36–38, 49, 54, 65–69, 72, 74–77, 79–80, 82, 100, 110, 112, 114, 133, 141–142, 144, 153–155, 161

sulphur dioxide an *oxide* of sulphur that helps to produce *acid rain* 101, 131–135

surveys a way of collecting *data*, for example by asking people questions or by looking at things and recording details about them 158

symbol a shorthand way of writing the names of *elements* 58–59, 62–64

symbol equation a *chemical equation* written using *symbols* 63, 102, 104–105, 107, 141

synthesis making new *molecules* 151

T

tarnish discoloration caused by the *reaction* of a *metal* with *oxygen* 111, 125

temperature a measure of the *heat energy* contained in hot objects 37, 46, 51–52, 78, 93–94, 98–99, 104, 137, 148, 157, 160, 162

texture describes rocks as *porous* or *non-porous* 78, 88, 90, 92

theory an idea to explain *evidence* 26–31, 38, 153–155, 163

thermal decomposition when a *compound* is broken down using heat 68

tissue a group of *cells* with the same shape and job

trend a pattern of results in a particular direction 134, 137, 162

trials testing of *drugs* and other chemicals before companies are allowed to sell them 151, 155

U

universal indicator an *indicator* that has many different colours depending on the *pH* of the *solution* that it is in 7–9, 14, 108–109, 112, 128

V

validity, of results whether results are *accurate*, measuring instruments are *precise* and used properly 158

variable in an experiment, something that can be changed to affect the result 157, 160, 162

variations, vary differences; to differ; to change something 77, 157, 160

vegetation cover the amount of plant growth in a place 126

vibrate to move from side to side 32, 37–38

volcanic ash *igneous rock* formed during explosive volcanic eruptions 95–96, 98

volcano mountain or hill formed from *lava* or ash during volcanic *eruptions* 95, 96, 98

voltage a measure of the amount of *energy* supplied to an *electric circuit* 146–147, 149, 155

W

water vapour water in the form of a *gas* 73, 76, 152–153

weathering breakdown of rock caused by rainwater and *temperature* changes 78–86, 88–89, 97–98, 126, 129, 140

word equation this shows the *reactants* and the products of a *chemical reaction* in words 16, 18–21, 24, 63, 67–68, 91, 102–105, 112, 115–116, 118, 141

Acknowledgements

We are grateful to the following for permission to reproduce photographs:

Alamy 99tr (Pictor/ImageState), 122m (Ethel Davies), 122bm (Leslie Garland); **Art Directors and Trip** 18l, 19tl, 19cl, 19bl, 21t, 21r, 21cl, 21cr, 145l (Helene Rogers); **British Geological Survey** 77b; **Catalyst Science Discovery Centre** 136b; **Corbis** 20t, 20b (Bettman), 22 (James Corwin), 54t (Thom Lang), 62 (Kevin Schafer), 77c (Michael St. Maur Sheil), 83b (Michael Busselle), 86t (Chinch Gryniewicz/Ecoscene), 93tl (Charles O'Rear), 96tr (Yann Arthus-Betrand), 106tl (Michael Freeman), 106tr (Marco Cauz), 106br (Ted Speigel), 115t (Galen Rowell), 119 (Robert Holmes), 122t (Michael S. Yamashita), 127b (Pat O'Hara), 129mt (David Muench), 133 (Document General Motors/Reuters), 135br (Steve Austin), 136l (Michael Maslan Historical Photographs), 136tr (Michael Nicholson), 143 (L.Clarke), 145r, 147l (Richard T. Nowitz), 147r (Adam Woolfit), 154 (Archivo Iconografico S.A.); **Ida Cook** 3r, 15t, 15l, 50; **Ecoscene** 131tr (Nick Hawkes), 134 (Vicki Coombs), 135m (l-r) (Chinch Gryniewicz), (Judyth Platt), (Sally Morgan), 144tr (Vicki Coombs); **Fisher Scientific** 162; **Geoscience Features Picture Library** 67b, 77l, 77r, 78m, 81tl, 81tr, 82t, 86b, 87m, 90l, 90r, 91bl, 92tr, 92ml, 92mr, 92bl, 92br, 94t, 94m, 94b, 95t, 95b, 96bl, 96br; **Griffin Education** 109; **Robert Harding** 70 (F. Friberg); **Philip Harris Education** 45; **Holt** 106tml (Inga Spence); **Andrew Lambert** 12b, 15cr, 15b, 17, 19br, 57bl, 79, 80, 91tr, 120 (all); **Nigel Luckhurst** 78t, 91br, 130tr; **Jean Martin** 157; **Vanessa Miles** 42, 53, 61, 83mt, 106tmr, 106bm, 115m, 126l, 126m, 129mb, 130tl, 130br, 153; **National Motor Museum** 21br; **Nature Picture Library** 126r (Premaphotos), 156 (Tony Heald); **Photofusion** 129b (Peter Olive); **Photos for Books** 10; **Professional Sport UK Ltd** 131tm (John Babb); **Science Photo Library** 12t (Prof. P. Motta), 18r (Dr Jeremy Burgess), 19tr (Martin Bond), 19cr (Jerry Mason), 27 (SPL), 29t (Northwestern University Library), 29b (SPL), 31 (US Library of Congress), 32 (Martin Dohrn), 54m (Pascal Goetgheluck), 54b (Claude Nuridsany and Marie Perennou), 57br (Charles D. Winters), 67t (Martyn F. Chillmaid), 67m (Charles D. Winters), 72tl (Tony McConnell), 72tr (Maximilian Stock Ltd), 72br (Simon Fraser), 73 (Charles D. Winters), 74 (David Taylor), 78b (Martin Bond), 82b (Sinclair Stammers), 86ml (Matthew Oldfield), 86mr (James King-Holmes), 87t (Nasa), 92tl (George Bernard), 93tr (G. Brad Lewis), 93br (Martin Bond), 95mt (Oscar Burriel), 95mb (Soames Summerhays), 99r (Simon Lewis), 99br (Charles D. Winters), 99bm (George Bernard), 99bl (Erich Schremp), 99ml (Sheila Terry), 99tl (Lawrence Lawry), 106bl (Dr Jeremy Burgess), 112t, 112b, 115b (Andrew Lambert), 118 (Jerry Mason), 121 (Sheila Terry), 122mt (Charles D. Winters), 122b (Alan Sirulnikoff), 127t (Martyn F. Chillmaid), 129t (Adam Hart-Davis), 131mb (Wesley Bocxe), 131bl (BSIP Chassenet), 131br (James King-Holmes), 142 (Richard Folwell), 144m (BSIP Chassenet), 144bl (Adam Hart-Davis), 144bm (Magrath Photography), 150l (Alfred Pasieka), 150r (Philippe Plailly); **Still Pictures** 13 (Mark Edwards), 144br (David Woodfall); **Wellcome Trust Medical Photographic Library** 3c; **Chris Westwood** 81br, 83mb; **Wilderness Photography** 83t.

Picture research: Vanessa Miles and Jacqui Rivers

We have made every effort to trace copyright holders, but if we have inadvertently overlooked any we will be pleased to make the necessary arrangements at the earliest opportunity.